GW01161416

CHICKEN DISHES
FROM
AROUND THE WORLD

GETTING IT RIGHT

CHICKEN DISHES FROM AROUND THE WORLD

by
Anne Chamberlain

Edited by
Christine Smeeth

foulsham
London · New York · Toronto · Sydney

foulsham

**The Publishing House, Bennetts Close,
Cippenham, Berkshire, SL1 5AP**

ISBN 0-572-02139-9

Printed in Great Britain at
Cox & Wayman Ltd, Reading, Berks.

CONTENTS

INTRODUCTION

Chicken is a wonderfully versatile food, and there are dozens of different ways of cooking it to give flavour and variety to the meals you cook. What used to be an expensive luxury served roasted as a special Sunday lunch, has now, with modern breeding methods become an everyday food. Birds are produced which compare favourably in price with other meat. Birds of every size are available and chicken joints, drumsticks and wings can be readily purchased to make a meal for any number of people.

In spite of lower prices, chicken still has an air of luxury because it marries with so many other tasty ingredients. A few mushrooms, a pinch of fresh herbs, and the addition of a spoonful of wine and cream can produce a gourmet dish. Chicken breast meat can be relied upon to be succulent and tender and a few slices of avocado, a splash of lemon juice and the addition of a pinch of marjoram provides an exotic touch to a recipe. On the other hand, a chicken prepared with root vegetables and a thick, rich gravy makes a satisfying and delicious meal for a hungry family. It is so often the addition of the little extras that make each dish a meal to remember.

The recipes in this book specify a bird of average weight, i.e. 1.5 kg (3 lb), as this is the size obtainable in most shops, supermarkets and freezer centres. Individual chicken breasts, drumsticks and wings are almost always obtainable. Poussins are small chickens, available from most large supermarkets. For a larger family a 2–2.5 kg (4½–5½ lb) chicken will produce a main meal, the leftovers often making a second-day dish possibly including soup and sandwiches as well. Chickens are usually sold trussed, that is, ready for the oven. When chicken joints are used, four will feed an average family, but recipes may be easily halved or doubled according to the size of the meal. Small 1.5 kg (3 lb) chickens may be easily jointed at home with a heavy sharp knife cutting the chicken in half through the breastbone, then dividing each half into two pieces, one larger piece with the majority of the breast and a smaller piece with the leg attached to it. The chicken can be divided into smaller sections if it is a big bird.

If a frozen chicken is used, it is important that the meat, whether it be a whole bird, joints, drumsticks or wings, is completely thawed before cooking. To do this place the meat in the refrigerator, still in its wrapping, and allow it to thaw slowly. Be sure to remove the giblets from inside the bird before cooking.

To make stock for soups, sauces and gravies, simmer the giblets in 1.2 ltrs/2 pints water with 1 onion, quartered, a large bunch of fresh herbs, salt and pepper and 1 carrot, chopped, for 2½ hours, then strain. When the main meal is over, remove all the remaining chicken flesh from the carcass and and store it in the refrigerator for another meal. You can also use the carcass, roughly chopped into four manageable pieces, for making stock as above. It will keep for up to 2 weeks when stored in the refrigerator. If you buy joints and don't make your own stock, just use a good quality stock cube.

To test a bird to see if it is cooked, pierce in several places with a skewer or a sharp knife. If the liquid that oozes out is clear, then the chicken is cooked.

A good roasted chicken deserves good carving. Use a really sharp knife, and carve first one side, then the other. Remove the whole leg from the bird and divide it into two portions: thigh and drumstick. Slice the breast vertically off the carcass, making each slice long enough to include some stuffing. Finally, take off the wing and serve whole.

ROAST CHICKEN

A whole chicken may be roasted very simply with herbs and seasoning for flavouring and just a little oil or butter for basting. Most people enjoy a stuffed chicken, so try corn and bacon stuffing: 25 g (1 oz/2 tbsp) butter, 1 onion, chopped, 75 g (3 oz/⅓ cup) bacon, chopped, 100 g (4 oz/1 cup) sweetcorn, drained, 15 ml (1 tbsp) thyme, chopped, salt and pepper, 225 g (8 oz/4 cups) breadcrumbs, 1 egg, beaten. Melt the butter in a saucepan and fry the onion and bacon for 3 minutes to soften. Place in a bowl, blend in the remaining ingredients and spoon into the bird. Or try a simple puréed chestnut and sausagemeat stuffing as a change from the traditional parsley and thyme, or sage and onion. Stuff a bird very lightly or the stuffing will become solid and unappetising during cooking.

To roast a chicken, rub salt, pepper and 15 ml (1 tbsp) butter over the bird. Stuff it as above, if desired, and place in a roasting pan. Cook at 200°C/400°F/gas mark 6 allowing 25 minutes per 450 g (1 lb) in weight plus 25 minutes for a stuffed bird. Traditional accompaniments for chicken include clear gravy, bread sauce, bacon rolls and chipolata sausages.

Orchard Chicken with Chestnut and Sage Stuffing

Serves 4

	Metric	Imperial	American
Chicken	1.5 kg	3 lb	3 lb
Seasoning			
Cooking apple, peeled	1	1	1
Onion	1	1	1
Oil	15 ml	1 tbsp	1 tbsp
Clear honey	60 ml	4 tbsp	4 tbsp
Chestnuts, peeled	550 g	1 ¼ lb	1 ¼ lb
Stock	450 ml	¾ pt	2 cups
Pork sausagemeat	225 g	8 oz	½ lb
Breadcrumbs	75 g	3 oz	1½ cups
Eggs, beaten	2	2	2
Butter	15 g	1 tbsp	1 tbsp

Remove the core from the apple and chop roughly. Slice the onion in half and set one half aside. Chop the other half of the onion and mix with the apple. Pack the apple and onion into the chicken.

Put the chestnuts, stock, salt and pepper in a saucepan and bring to the boil. Lower the heat and simmer for 1 hour, until the chestnuts are soft and the stock has been absorbed. Transfer to a bowl and allow to cool for 10 minutes. Mash the chestnuts.

Melt the butter in the saucepan and chop the other half of the onion. Fry with the sausage meat for 8 minutes. Remove from the heat and blend into the chestnuts. Mix in the breadcrumbs and eggs and spoon into the chicken.

Brush the chicken with the oil and place into a roasting pan. Pour over the honey and roast at 190°C/375°F/gas mark 5 for 1 hour 55 minutes, basting from time to time with the pan juices. Serve with boiled new potatoes and a green vegetable.

Roast Chicken
with Port Thyme Gravy

Serves 4

	Metric	Imperial	American
Chicken	1.5 kg	3 lb	3 lb
Butter	30 ml	2 tbsp	2 tbsp
Seasoning			
Onion, chopped	1	1	1
Carrots, chopped	3	3	3
Thyme, chopped	6 sprigs	6 sprigs	6 sprigs
Bay leaves	2	2	2
Stock	300 ml	½ pt	1 ¼ cups
Port	120 ml	4 fl oz	½ cup
Cornflour (cornstarch)	30 ml	2 tbsp	2 tbsp
Oil	15 ml	1 tbsp	1 tbsp

Rub the butter over the chicken and sprinkle with salt and pepper. Pour over the oil and place the chicken in a pan and cook at 220°C/425°F/gas mark 7 for 20 minutes. Lower the heat to 200°C/400°F/gas mark 6 and continue cooking for 1 hour 15 minutes.

Remove the chicken from the pan and keep warm, then reheat the oil and fry the onions and carrots for 5 minutes. Add the thyme, bay leaf and stock to the onions and bring to the boil. Lower the heat and simmer for 55 minutes. Blend the port with the cornflour and stir into the stock. Remove the bay leaves and serve with the roast meat.

Sweetcorn Chicken

Serves 4

	Metric	Imperial	American
Chicken	*1.5 kg*	*3 lb*	*3 lb*
Butter	*25 g*	*1 oz*	*2 tbsp*
Onion	*1*	*1*	*1*
Seasoning	*1.5 ml*	*¼ tsp*	*¼ tsp*
Canned sweetcorn			
* kernels*	*150 g*	*5 oz*	*1¼ cups*
Grated rind of lemon	*½*	*½*	*½*
Squeeze of lemon juice			
Chopped parsley	*15 ml*	*1 tbsp*	*1 tbsp*
Egg, beaten	*1*	*1*	*1*

Melt the butter in a saucepan, add the chopped onion and cook over a gentle heat until it begins to soften. Stir in the seasoning and sweetcorn and cook for 2–3 minutes. Remove from the heat, add the grated lemon rind and juice, the parsley and beaten egg. Mix thoroughly and spoon loosely into the bird. Roast at 180°C/350°F/ gas mark 4 for 1½ hours.

Somerset Chicken

Serves 4

	Metric	Imperial	American
Chicken	1.5 kg	3 lb	3 lb
Soft dark brown sugar	15 g	1 tbsp	1 tbsp
Grated lemon rind	½	½	½
Lemon juice	5 ml	1 tsp	1 tsp
Butter	25 g	1 oz	2 tbsp
Cooking apples	225 g	8 oz	½ lb
Cider	150 ml	¼ pt	⅔ cup
Cornflour or cornstarch	10 ml	2 tsp	2 tsp
Water	30 ml	2 tbsp	2 tbsp
Salt and pepper			
Stuffing			
Breadcrumbs	175 g	6 oz	3 cups
Juice of 1 lemon	1	1	1
Chopped, fresh parsley	60 ml	4 tbsp	4 tbsp
Chopped, fresh thyme	15 ml	1 tbsp	1tbsp
Butter	50 g	2 oz	¼ cup
Eggs	2	2	2

To make the stuffing, blend together the stuffing ingredients and spoon into the chicken cavity.

Mix together the sugar, lemon rind and juice and butter, and spread the mixture on the breast of the chicken. Roast at 190°C/375°F/gas mark 5, basting frequently for 1¼ hours. Peel and core the apples and cut them into rings. Put the apple rings round the chicken and pour the cider over the bird. Continue cooking for 20 minutes. Put the chicken and apple rings onto a serving dish.

Mix the cornflour and water until smooth and add to the pan juices. Stir well, season and bring to the boil. Serve each portion of chicken with some apple rings, stuffing and cider sauce.

Pineapple Stuffed Chicken

Serves 4

	Metric	Imperial	American
Chicken	1.5 kg	3 lb	3 lb
Butter	50 g	2 oz	¼ cup
Stuffing			
Onion, chopped	1	1	1
Butter	25 g	1 oz	2 tbsp
Stale white breadcrumbs	100 g	4 oz	2 cups
Walnuts, chopped	50 g	2 oz	½ cup
Seedless raisins	50 g	2 oz	⅓ cup
Grated lemon rind	½	½	½
Seasoning			
Canned pineapple slices	225 g	8 oz	½ lb
Extra walnut halves for garnishing			
Stock	150 ml	¼ pt	⅔ cup

Remove the giblets from the chicken and make a stock (see page 7). To make the stuffing, fry the onion in the butter without letting it brown. Stir in the breadcrumbs, walnuts, raisins and lemon rind and season well. Drain two of the pineapple slices and chop them roughly. Add to the stuffing with 1 tbsp juice to bind and pack into the neck or body of the bird. Do not pack too tightly as the stuffing swells during cooking. Secure the neck flap in position under the wing tips. Place in a roasting tin, spread with butter and cover with buttered paper. Cook at 180°C/350°F/gas mark 4 for 1¼ hours. The stock can be used to make the gravy or kept in the refrigerator for soups or casseroles, ensuring the fat has been removed once the liquid has cooled.

When cooked, put the bird on a serving dish. Add a little stock to the tin and make gravy in the usual way. Heat the remaining pineapple slices in their juice and arrange them round the bird. Garnish with some walnut halves and serve with baked jacket potatoes and a green vegetable.

Roast Chicken with Orange and Chestnut Stuffing

Serves 4

	Metric	Imperial	American
Chicken	1.5 kg	3 lb	3 lb
Butter	50 g	2 oz	¼ cup
Stuffing			
Onion, chopped	1	1	1
Butter	25 g	1 oz	2 tbsp
Long-grain rice	100 g	4 oz	½ cup
Oranges	2	2	2
Skinned chestnuts	225 g	8 oz	1 cup
Seasoning			
Bay leaf	1	1	1
Egg, beaten	1	1	1

Remove the giblets from the chicken and make stock for later use (see page 7). To make the stuffing, chop the onion and gently fry in the butter until soft. Boil the rice in plenty of salted water, drain and rinse well. Mix it with the onion. Halve each orange and cut out the flesh with a grapefruit knife. Remove all white pith and add the segments to the rice mixture.

Roughly chop the chestnuts, mix together with the seasonings and bay leaf, and bind with the egg. Pack into the body cavity of the bird. Secure the neck flap in position under the wing tips. Spread the butter over the chicken, and cover with buttered paper. Place in a roasting tin. Cook at 180°C/350°F/gas mark 4 for 1¼ hours.

Fruit and Nut Chicken

Serves 4

	Metric	Imperial	American
Chicken	1.5 kg	3 lb	3 lb
Butter	50 g	2 oz	¼ cup
Grated orange rind	1	1	1
Tabasco sauce	1.5 ml	¼ tsp	¼ tsp
Stuffing			
Butter	25 g	1 oz	2 tbsp
Onion, chopped	1	1	1
Cooked rice	100 g	4 oz	1 cup
Liver sausage	100 g	4 oz	1 cup
Raisins	50 g	2 oz	⅓ cup
Almonds	50 g	2 oz	½ cup
Egg	1	1	1
Tabasco sauce	3.5 ml	¾ tsp	¾ tsp
Seasoning			

To make the stuffing, fry the chopped onion gently in the butter until soft, but not browned. Put the onion, rice, liver sausage, raisins and almonds into a basin. Beat the egg with the Tabasco sauce, salt and pepper. Add the egg to the stuffing and mix well together. Stuff the chicken in the usual way. Cream the butter with orange rind and Tabasco sauce. Spread the butter mixture over the chicken. Roast at 190°C/375°F/gas mark 5 for 1½ hours.

GRILLED OR FRIED CHICKEN

Chicken joints provide the basis of many quick-to-prepare grilled and fried meals. Use all parts of the bird, breast, drumsticks, wings, etc. For range and variety. One chicken joint serves each person generously and can be served with vegetables, rice, pasta or salad. Grilled and fried chicken joints are also delicious for barbecues and can be eaten cold. They make ideal buffet dishes or easy-to-eat portions for a picnic.

Cold Spicy Chicken

Serves 4

	Metric	Imperial	American
Chicken joints	4	4	4
Chicken stock	150 ml	¼ pt	⅔ cup
Turmeric	5 ml	1 tsp	1 tsp
Mild curry powder	5 ml	1 tsp	1 tsp
Ground ginger	5 ml	1 tsp	1 tsp
Mustard powder	5 ml	1 tsp	1 tsp
Pepper	2.5 ml	½ tsp	½ tsp
Mixed herbs	2.5 ml	½ tsp	½ tsp
Ground mixed spice	1.5 ml	¼ tsp	¼ tsp
Butter	25 g	1 oz	2 tbsp
Mango chutney			

Poach the joints in the stock for about 20 minutes or until tender. blend the herbs and spices together. Drain the chicken, reserving the stock to make soup. Pat the joints dry on kitchen paper. Sprinkle the herb and spice mixture over the joints and leave for 30 minutes. Brush the chicken with melted butter and put under the grill until they turn golden brown and crisp, turning and basting frequently. Leave to cool. Serve with mango chutney.

Creamy Ginger Chicken

Serves 4

	Metric	Imperial	American
Chicken joints	4	4	4
Seasoning			
Chopped fresh tarragon	5 ml	1 tsp	1 tsp
Ginger, peeled and grated	100 g	4 oz	1 cup
Olive oil	30 ml	2 tbsp	2 tbsp
Crème fraîche	450 g	1 lb	2 cups
Spring onions (scallions)	4	4	4

Season the chicken with salt and pepper. Blend the tarragon with the ginger and olive oil and spread over the chicken. Place in a steamer and cook for 30 minutes or until tender. Remove the chicken pieces and place them on a warm serving dish. Stir in enough cooking juices from the steamer to thin the créme fraîche to the consistency of single cream. Chop the spring onions and fold into the créme fraîche. Spoon the sauce over the warm chicken and serve immediately.

Rich Golden Grilled Chicken

Serves 4

	Metric	Imperial	American
Chicken joints	4	4	4
Lemon	1	1	1
Salt			
Melted butter	50 g	2 oz	¼ cup
Sugar	25 g	1 oz	2 tbsp
Paprika	1.5 ml	¼ tsp	¼ tsp

Pierce the lemon a few times then, squeeze a little to release the juice, sprinkle all over the chicken. Sprinkle the chicken lightly with salt then brush liberally on both sides with melted butter. Place cut side uppermost in the bottom of the grill pan (grid removed), and cook under a medium heat for 10–12 minutes. Turn skin side uppermost and sprinkle evenly with mixed sugar and paprika. Continue grilling for a further 10–15 minutes, or until the juices run clear when pierced with a sharp knife. Brush frequently with melted butter. Serve with fresh green broccoli and carrot straws.

Barbecued Chicken Grill

Serves 4

	Metric	Imperial	American
Chicken joints	4	4	4
Butter	50 g	2 oz	4 tbsp
Malt vinegar	60 ml	4 tbsp	4 tbsp
Worcestershire sauce	15 ml	1 tbsp	1 tbsp
Tomato purée	15 ml	1 tbsp	1 tbsp
Brown sugar	25 g	1 oz	2 tbsp
Finely grated onion	5 ml	1 tsp	1 tsp
Paprika	5 ml	1 tsp	1 tsp
Salt	2.5 ml	½ tsp	½ tsp
Chopped fresh chives			

Melt the butter in a small saucepan and brush liberally all over the chicken. Arrange skin side down in the grill pan (rack removed), and grill it gently for 12–15 minutes. Meanwhile make the barbecue sauce by adding all the remaining ingredients, except the chives to the butter in the saucepan and simmering together for two minutes. Turn the chicken skin side up, brush with barbecue sauce and continue grilling it gently, basting with the sauce, for a further 12–15 minutes. To serve, pour the remaining sauce over the chicken and garnish with the chives. Serve with crusty bread and butter.

Devilled Chicken

Serves 4

	Metric	Imperial	American
Chicken joints	4	4	4
Plain (all-purpose) flour	50 g	2 oz	½ cup
Salt	7½ ml	1½ tsp	1½ tsp
Mustard powder	10 ml	2 tsp	2 tsp
Egg, beaten	1	1	1
Water	15 ml	1 tbsp	1 tbsp
Fine semolina	75 g	3 oz	½ cup
Oil for frying			

Mix the flour, salt and mustard and coat each chicken joint. Dip the joints in the combined egg and water and drain each piece well in a sieve or colander. Allow to stand for 15–20 minutes. Dip into the semolina, turning the chicken so all parts are covered. Let it stand again for a few minutes and shake off any loose semolina.

Heat the oil until hot but not smoking. Brown the chicken pieces quickly, covering the pan with a lid for the first half of the cooking time (about 12 minutes). For a really crisp finish remove the lid for the last 10–12 minutes cooking time. Serve hot with mashed potatoes and a green vegetable, or serve cold with potato salad, green salad and tomatoes.

Chicken and Lentil Burgers

Serves 4

	Metric	Imperial	American
Minced chicken	350 g	12 oz	1½ cups
Red lentils	100 g	4 oz	⅔ cup
Breadcrumbs	50 g	2 oz	1 cup
Lemon juice	1 tbsp	1 tbsp	1 tbsp
Oregano, chopped	5 ml	1 tsp	1 tsp
Seasoning			
Oil for frying			

Place the lentils in a saucepan of boiling water and cook for 30 minutes or until soft. Drain and place in a bowl with the remaining ingredients. Blend well. Shape into 4 round burgers. Heat the oil in a shallow frying pan and cook the burgers gently for 8 minutes. Turn and cook the other side for 6 minutes or until brown and cooked right through.

Crunchy Crisp Baked Chicken

Sereves 4

	Metric	Imperial	American
Chicken joints	4	4	4
Plain (all-purpose) flour	25 g	1 oz	2 tbsp
Salt	5 ml	1 tsp	1 tsp
Curry powder	2.5 ml	½ tsp	½ tsp
Evaporated milk	120 ml	4 fl oz	½ cup
Potato crisps	75 g	3 oz	⅔ cup

Pre-heat the oven to 180°C/350°F/gas mark 4. Mix the flour, salt and curry powder together. Put the potato crisps into a bag then crush with a rolling pin. Coat the chicken joints with the seasoned flour, then dip them in the milk and coat thickly and evenly with the potato crisp crumbs. Arrange skin side up on a baking sheet and bake for about 40 minutes. Serve hot or cold with a green salad and a minted yoghurt dressing.

Fried Chicken with Lemon Rice

Serves 4

	Metric	Imperial	American
Chicken joints	4	4	4
Plain (all-purpose) flour	50 g	2 oz	½ cup
Salt	5 ml	1 tsp	1 tsp
Mild curry powder	10 ml	2 tsp	2 tsp
Oil for frying			
Bananas, cut into chunks	2	2	2
Long-grain rice	225 g	8 oz	1 cup
Lemon	1	1	1
Lemon juice	5 ml	1 tsp	1 tsp
Sultanas	50 g	2 oz	⅓ cup
Butter	50 g	2 oz	¼ cup
Grated rind of lemon	10 ml	2 tsp	2 tsp

Mix together the flour, salt and curry powder and coat the chicken joints with the mixture. Fry them in oil, turning once or twice, for about 10 minutes until golden. Reduce the heat, cover the pan and cook for 15 minutes until tender. Add the bananas and continue cooking for 5 minutes. Meanwhile boil the rice in salted water for 15 minutes, adding a slice of lemon. Stir in the lemon juice and sultanas and continue cooking for 8–10 minutes until the rice is soft. Drain and remove lemon slice. Stir in butter and 2 tsp grated rind from part of the lemon. Spread the rice on a serving dish, arrange chicken and banana pieces on top and garnish with the remaining lemon cut into slices.

Cheesey Drumsticks

Serves 4

	Metric	Imperial	American
Chicken drumsticks	8	8	8
Fine white breadcrumbs	100 g	4 oz	2 cups
cheese, finely grated	50 g	2 oz	½ cup
Chopped fresh parsley	10 ml	2 tsp	2 tsp
Onion, finely chopped	1	1	1
Seasoning			
Plain (all-purpose) flour	50 g	2 oz	½ cup
Egg	1	1	1
Oil for deep frying			

Mix together the breadcrumbs, cheese, parsley and onion and season with salt and pepper. Season the flour with salt and pepper and coat the drumsticks with the seasoned flour. Dip them in beaten egg and then coat the drumsticks in the breadcrumb mixture. Repeat this coating process with all the drumsticks then deep-fry them in hot oil for 10–15 minutes or until they are crisp and golden. Drain on kitchen paper. Serve hot with an apple sauce, baked tomatoes and new potatoes, or cold with salad.

CASSEROLES AND BAKES

Whole chicken and chicken pieces are very versatile and may be cooked in a casserole or baked in a sauce. The flavour of these dishes is best if the chicken is lightly fried first in a mixture of oil and butter, which seals the flesh and keeps the chicken juicy and full of flavour. Mushrooms, onions, carrots and tomatoes are natural partners to a casserole and the addition of a little wine will give a lift to the dish, imparting a Continental flavour. Garlic, once favoured mostly by European chefs, has at last been accepted by the British, with the realisation that a single crushed clove imparts and brings out the true flavours of a casserole.

Baked Barbecued Chicken

Serves 4

	Metric	Imperial	American
Chicken joints	4	4	4
Lemon juice	30 ml	2 tbsp	2 tbsp
Oil	45 ml	3 tbsp	3 tbsp
Worcestershire sauce	15 ml	1 tbsp	1 tbsp
Tabasco sauce	10 drops	10 drops	10 drops
Garlic clove	1	1	1
Tomato sauce	15 ml	1 tbsp	1 tbsp
Black pepper			
Oil for frying			
Butter	15 ml	1 tbsp	1 tbsp
Seasoned flour	45 ml	3 tbsp	3 tbsp
Tomatoes, chopped	6	6	6

Make deep cuts with a pointed knife into the flesh of the chicken. Mix together all the other ingredients except the oil, butter, tomatoes and flour. Pour the mixture over the chicken and refrigerate for some hours or overnight. Lift the joints from the marinade, roll them in seasoned flour, and sear in the oil in a flameproof casserole then bake at 190°C/375°F/gas mark 5 for 30 minutes, turning half-way through. Heat the butter in a saucepan and add the remaining seasoned flour. Cook for 30 seconds and gradually stir in the remaining marinade. Blend well and pour in the chopped tomatoes. Cook slowly, until the sauce thickens. Pour over the chicken joints before serving.

Farmhouse Chicken Bake

Serves 4

	Metric	Imperial	American
Chicken	1.5 kg	3 lb	3 lb
Seasoned flour	15 g	½ oz	1 tbsp
Rashers streaky bacon or slices bacon	4	4	4
Cider	30 ml	2 tbsp	2 tbsp
Seasoning			
Fresh white breadcrumbs	225 g	8 oz	4 cups
Shredded suet or finely chopped suet	100 g	4 oz	1 cup
Onions, finely chopped	2	2	2
Sprig of rosemary			
Grated rind of ½ lemon			
Egg	1	1	1
A little milk			

Cut the chicken into 8 pieces, toss them in the seasoned flour and place in a casserole. Cover with the bacon rashers and pour the cider over. Season. Mix all the other ingredients together adding enough milk to bind. Cover the chicken with this mixture to form a crust, pressing down evenly. Cover and bake at 180°C/350°F/gas mark 4 for 2 hours. Remove the lid and cook for a further 15 minutes to brown the crust.

Chicken Mornay

Serves 4

	Metric	Imperial	American
Chicken	1.5 kg	3 lb	3 lb
Chicken stock	600 ml	1 pt	2½ cups
Peppercorns	6	6	6
Bayleaf	1	1	1
Sprig of rosemary			
Noodles	225 g	8 oz	2 cups
Butter	25 g	1 oz	2 tbsp
Plain (all-purpose) flour	25 g	1 oz	2 tbsp
Milk	600 ml	1 pt	2½ cups
Seasoning			
Grated cheese	175 g	6 oz	1½ cups
Caraway seeds	10 ml	2 tsp	2 tsp
Extra butter			

Wash the chicken inside and out, then place in a large saucepan and poach gently in the stock with the peppercorns, bayleaf and rosemary for about 1 hour or until tender. Boil the noodles in salted water for about 10 minutes or until tender. Melt the butter in a pan and stir in the flour and cook gently for 1 minute. Gradually blend in the milk, then thicken it over a moderate heat. Season and add the cheese. Drain the noodles and toss them in a little butter with the caraway seeds. Arrange on a serving dish then place the chicken on top of the noodles and coat with the sauce. Put under the grill for a few minutes until the sauce starts to turn golden. Do not allow to burn.

Country Chicken Dumpling Roll

Serves 4

	Metric	Imperial	American
Self-raising (self-rising) flour or plain flour (all-purpose) sifted with 4 tsp baking powder	450 g	1 lb	4 cups
Salt	5 ml	1 tsp	1 tsp
Shredded suet	150 g	5 oz	1¼ cup
Cooked chicken, chopped	225 g	8 oz	½ lb
Chicken livers	225 g	8 oz	½ lb
Mushrooms	225 g	8 oz	½ lb
Dried marjoram	15 ml	1 tbsp	1 tbsp
Seasoning			
Mushroom sauce			
Butter	50 g	2 oz	¼ cup
Mushrooms, sliced	225 g	8 oz	½ lb
Cornflour (cornstarch)	10 ml	2 tsp	2 tsp
Chicken stock	300 ml	½ pt	1¼ cups
Seasoning			
Tomato purée	10 ml	1 tsp	1 tsp

To make the, dumpling roll mix the flour, salt and suet with cold water to form a firm pastry. Roll into a rectangle. Cover with the cooked chicken and the cooked chicken livers, the mushrooms, marjoram and seasoning. Roll up and put on baking sheet. Bake at 190°C/375°F/gas mark 5 for 45 minutes.

To make the sauce, heat the butter and lightly fry the mushrooms for about 4 minutes. Blend the cornflour with a little stock then add to the pan and cook for 2 minutes, stirring continuously. Add the remaining stock, season and bring to the boil. Add the tomato purèe and cook for a further 2 minutes, stirring well.

Serve the dumpling roll with the mushroom sauce poured over or handed separately in a sauce boat.

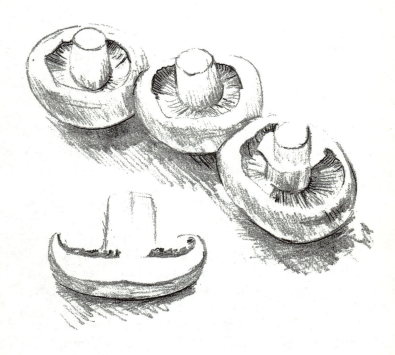

Cheesey Chicken Crumble

Serves 4

	Metric	Imperial	American
Onion, finely chopped	1	1	1
Butter	25 g	1 oz	2 tbsp
Plain (all-purpose) flour	25 g	1 oz	¼ cup
Milk	150 ml	¼ pt	⅔ cup
Chicken stock (made from a cube)	150 ml	¼ pt	⅔ cup
Cooked chicken	350 g	12 oz	3 cups
Seasoning			
Worcestershire sauce	5 ml	1 tsp	1 tsp
Tomatoes, sliced	2	2	2
Topping			
Plain (all-purpose) flour	75 g	3 oz	¾ cup
Pinch of salt			
Butter	40 g	1½ oz	3 tbsp
Cheddar cheese	50 g	2 oz	½ cup

Fry the onion in the butter until soft but not brown. Stir in the flour and cook for 1 minute. Remove from the heat and gradually stir in the milk and stock. Return to the heat, then bring to the boil, stirring, and cook for 1 minute. Dice the chicken, and add to the pan with the seasoning and Worcestershire sauce. Put the chicken into an ovenware dish. Place slices of tomato on top of the chicken mixture. Sieve the flour and salt into a bowl and rub in the butter until the mixture resembles fine breadcrumbs. Stir in the grated cheese. Spoon this crumble over the tomatoes. Bake at 190°C/375°F/gas mark 5 for 40 minutes.

Ginger Chicken

Serves 4

	Metric	Imperial	American
Chicken joints	4	4	4
Butter	100 g	4 oz	½ cup
Onions, sliced	2	2	2
Made mustard seasoning	30 ml	2 tbsp	2 tbsp
Orange juice	30 ml	2 tbsp	2 tbsp
Walnut sized piece of ginger, finely chopped			
Stock	300 ml	½ pt	1¼ cups

Melt the butter in a large pan and brown the chicken joints all over. Remove from the pan and set aside to cool slightly. Add the onions to the pan and fry gently until soft. Coat the chicken with mustard, season and return to the pan. Add the orange juice, stock and ginger. Bring to the boil then simmer for 45 minutes stirring occasionally.

Chiswick Chicken

Serves 4

	Metric	Imperial	American
Chicken joints	4	4	4
Butter	50 g	2 oz	¼ cup
Tomatoes, skinned and chopped	225 g	8 oz	2 cups
Spring onions (scallions), chopped	4	4	4
Plain (all-purpose) flour	25 g	1 oz	2 tbsp
Milk	150 ml	¼ pt	⅔ cup
Curry powder	5 ml	1 tsp	1 tsp
Seasoning			
Cooked green peas	50 g	2 oz	½ cup
Mushrooms	100 g	4 oz	2 cups
Soured (dairy sour) cream	150 ml	¼ pt	⅔ cup
Chopped fresh parsley			

Cook the chicken joints in ½ pt/300 ml boiling water for 25 minutes or until tender. Allow to cool for 10 minutes and drain thoroughly, reserving the cooling liquor. Skin and strip the meat from the bones and tear the meat into large pieces. Melt the butter and cook the tomatoes and spring onions until soft and golden. Stir in the flour and gradually stir in the milk with ¼ pt/ 150 ml of the chicken cooking liquor. Stir over a low heat until a creamy sauce has formed. Add the curry powder, and seasoning, and then stir in the peas and sliced mushrooms. Heat gently and stir in the soured cream and chicken pieces. Do not boil once the cream has been added. Serve garnished with the chopped parsley.

Vineyard Chicken

Serves 4

	Metric	Imperial	American
Chicken joints	4	4	4
Onion, chopped	1	1	1
Mushrooms	175 g	6 oz	3 cups
Carrots	225 g	8 oz	2 cups
Seasoned flour	15 g	½ oz	1 tbsp
White wine	150 ml	¼ pt	⅔ cup
Chicken stock	300 ml	½ pt	1¼ cups
Tomato purée	15 ml	1 tbsp	1 tbsp
Salt and pepper			

Place the chicken joints, onion, sliced mushrooms and carrots in an ovenproof dish. Add the seasoned flour and mix well. Blend the wine and stock with the tomato purèe and pour it over the chicken and vegetables. Season and bake at 180°C/350°F/gas mark 4 for 1½ hours.

Tarragon Chicken

Serves 4

	Metric	Imperial	American
Chicken	1.5 kg	3 lb	3 lb
Butter	25 g	1 oz	2 tbsp
Carrots, thinly sliced	2	2	2
Onion, thinly sliced	1	1	1
Stick of celery or stalk of celery, thinly sliced	1	1	1
Parsley sprigs	4	4	4
Chicken stock	1 litre	1¾ pts	4½ cups
Tarragon	1.5 ml	½ tsp	½ tsp
Clove	1	1	1
Pinch of salt			
Egg yolks	2	2	2

Fry the carrots, onions and celery with the butter in a pan. Cover and cook very gently for 30 minutes. Put the vegetables in a casserole with the parsley on top. Put the chicken on the vegetables and cover with boiling stock. Add the tarragon, clove and pinch of salt. Cover and cook at 180°C/350°F/gas mark 4 for 1½ hours. Drain the chicken liquid reserving 600 ml (1 pt/2½ cups) cooking liquor. Put the measured stock into a saucepan and boil rapidly until the liquid has reduced by half. Take off the heat and pour a little of the hot liquid on to the egg yolks. Whisk together quickly and stir in the remaining hot liquid. Pour over the chicken before serving.

Devonshire Chicken Casserole

Serves 4

	Metric	Imperial	American
Chicken joints	4	4	4
Butter	50 g	2 oz	1/4 cup
Onion	50 g	2 oz	1/2 cup
Stick of celery	1	1	1
Rashers (slices) streaky bacon	2	2	2
Plain (all-purpose) flour	25 g	1 oz	1/4 cup
Pepper	1.5 ml	1/4 tsp	1/4 tsp
Chicken stock	450 ml	3/4 pt	2 cups
Tomatoes	3	3	3

Fry the chicken joints in the butter over a gentle heat for 10 minutes. Put the chicken into a casserole. Chop the onion, celery and bacon and cook them in the butter for 5 minutes. Sprinkle in the flour and pepper. Stir for a minute over heat then blend in the stock. Skin the tomatoes, remove the seeds, and cut the flesh in quarters. Add the tomatoes to the sauce and pour it over the chicken. Cover and cook at 180°C/350°F/ gas mark 4 for 45 minutes. Serve with mashed potatoes and peas.

Chicken in the Pot

Serves 4

	Metric	Imperial	American
Chicken	1.5 kg	3 lb	3 lb
Seasoning			
Sausage meat	100 g	4 oz	1 cup
Fresh breadcrumbs	15 ml	1 tbsp	1 tbsp
Chicken liver	1	1	1
Chopped fresh oregano	15 ml	1 tbsp	1 tbsp
Butter	50 g	2 oz	¼ cup
Oil	15 ml	1 tbsp	1 tbsp
Streaky bacon rashers, (slices) chopped	100 g	4 oz	⅔ cup
Button onions	12	12	12
Potatoes	450 g	1 lb	1 lb

Remove the giblets from inside the chicken, rinse then season the chicken inside and out with salt and pepper. Mix together the sausage meat, breadcrumbs, chopped liver and oregano and stuff the neck of the bird with it, securing the flap of skin under the wing tips. Heat the butter and oil in a flameproof casserole and brown the chicken all over. Add the chopped bacon and whole onions, cover closely and cook over a very gentle heat for 15 minutes. Baste the chicken, add the potatoes cut into small cubes and turn them in the fat. Continue cooking, covered in the oven pre-heated to 180°C/350°F/gas mark 4 for 1½ hours. Serve in the casserole, the potatoes sprinkled with chopped herbs.

Stoved Chicken

Serves 4

	Metric	Imperial	American
Onions, sliced	2	2	2
Potatoes	1 kg	2¼ lb	2¼ lb
Chicken joints	4	4	4
Butter	50 g	2 oz	¼ cup
Seasoning			
Chicken stock	600 ml	1 pt	2½ cups
Chopped fresh parsley	15 ml	1 tbsp	1 tbsp

Cut the potatoes into medium–thick slices. Brown the chicken joints in a frying pan in half the butter. Make a thick layer of a third of the potatoes in the bottom of the casserole, then add a layer of onions (using about half) and then the chicken joints. Season well with salt and pepper and dot with the remaining butter. Top with another layer of potatoes, then the remaining onions and finally potatoes. Season with salt, pepper and the chopped parsley and pour over the stock. Put on a piece of buttered greaseproof paper and a lid. Cook at 150°C/300°F/ gas mark 2 for 2½ hours.

Creamed Almond Chicken

Serves 4

	Metric	Imperial	American
Chicken	1.5 kg	3 lb	3 lb
Plain (all-purpose) flour	25 g	1 oz	1/4 cup
Seasoning			
Butter	25 g	1 oz	2 tbsp
Blanched almonds	25 g	1 oz	1/4 cup
Sticks of celery	2	2	2
Chicken stock	150 ml	1/4 pt	2/3 cup
Soured (dairy sour) cream	30 ml	2 tbsp	2 tbsp

Season the flour with salt and pepper and use to dust the chicken. Melt the butter in a frying pan and brown the chicken quickly on all sides. Cut the almonds into strips and cook them in the fat until they are golden. Put the chicken, almonds and chopped celery into a casserole dish with the chicken stock and salt and pepper to taste. Cover and cook at 190°C/375°F/gas mark 5 for 1 hour. Remove the lid and skim off the excess fat. Stir the cream into the pan juices and baste the chicken. Continue cooking for 15 minutes. Serve with rice.

Chicken and Mushroom Casserole

Serves 4

	Metric	Imperial	American
Chicken joints	4	4	4
Onion	1	1	1
Mushrooms	100 g	4 oz	2 cups
Butter	50 g	2 oz	¼ cup
Plain (all-purpose) flour	15 g	1 tbsp	1 tbsp
Salt and pepper			
Chopped fresh mixed herbs	5 ml	1 tsp	1 tsp
Tomato purée	30 ml	2 tbsp	2 tbsp
Chicken stock	600 ml	1 pt	2½ cups

Chop the onion and slice the mushrooms into quarters and fry them gently in the butter in a flameproof casserole until the onion is soft and golden. Add the chicken to the casserole and brown, then remove the joints and keep them warm. Sprinkle in the flour and seasonings and stir well. Add the herbs and the tomato purèe. Add the stock, stirring slowly until the mixture thickens. Return the chicken joints to the casserole, cover and simmer for 45 minutes, turning the chicken pieces once during cooking.

Pot Roast Chicken

Serves 4

	Metric	Imperial	American
Chicken	1.5 kg	3 lb	3 lb
Butter	40 g	1½ oz	3 tbsp
Sticks of celery, sliced	2	2	2
Onions, sliced	6	6	6
Carrots, sliced	2	2	2
Turnip, sliced	1	1	1
Chicken stock	300 ml	½ pt	1¼ cups
seasoning			
Chopped fresh parsley	15 ml	1 tbsp	1 tbsp

Brown the chicken lightly on all sides in the butter in a flameproof casserole. Add the sliced vegetables, stock and seasoning. Cover and simmer for 2 hours, basting occasionally with the stock. Garnish with the parsley before serving. If preferred, the chicken may be cooked in the oven at 180°C/350°F/gas mark 4.

Chicken Robert

Serves 4

	Metric	Imperial	American
Chicken joints	4	4	4
plain (all-purpose) flour	15 g	½ oz	1 tbsp
Butter	75 g	3 oz	6 tbsp
Prunes (soaked and stoned)	8	8	8
Canned tomatoes	225 g	8 oz	1 cup
Chicken stock cube	1	1	1
White wine	375 ml	13 fl oz	1½ cups
Bay leaf	1	1	1
Parsley sprigs	3	3	3
Shelled prawns	75 g	3 oz	¾ cup
Button mushrooms	100 g	4 oz	2 cups
Double (heavy) cream	15 ml	1 tbsp	1 tbsp

Coat the chicken in the flour then brown it on all sides in 2 tbsp butter in a frying pan. Remove the chicken to a casserole dish and add the prunes and tomatoes. Tie the bay leaf and parsley sprigs together with cotton and add them to the casserole with the stock cube and wine. Cover and cook in a pre-heated oven at 160°C/325°F/gas mark 3 for 1¼ hours. Add the prawns and continue cooking for another 5 minutes. Remove the bay leaf and parsley, test the seasoning then transfer the chicken to a serving dish. Sautè the mushrooms in 1 tbsp butter. Pour the sauce over the chicken and garnish with the sautèd mushrooms and with a little cream drizzled over.

Covent Garden Chicken

Serves 4

	Metric	Imperial	American
Chicken	1.5 kg	3 lb	3 lb
Seasoning			
Butter	100 g	4 oz	½ cup
Baby carrots	12	12	12
Baby white turnips	4	4	4
Sugar	5 ml	1 tsp	1 tsp
Baby onions	8	8	8
Small new potatoes	8	8	8
Lean bacon, chopped	100 g	4 oz	⅔ cup
Chicken stock	150 ml	¼ pt	⅔ cup
White wine	150 ml	¼ pt	⅔ cup

Season the chicken with salt and pepper. Melt half the butter in a large frying pan and turn the chicken in the butter to brown evenly. Transfer the bird to a casserole dish. Cut the carrots and turnips into quaters. Melt the remaining butter in another pan and gently fry the carrots and turnips in the butter with the sugar for 2–3 minutes. Add the peeled whole onions, potatoes and chopped bacon and cook for a further 3 minutes. Turn all the vegetables into the casserole, add the stock and wine then cover and cook in a pre-heated oven at 200°C/400°F/gas mark 6 for 1½ hours. Lift the chicken out of the casserole, joint it and return it to the dish. Serve with a green salad and French bread.

INTERNATIONAL CHICKEN

Chicken is popular in every country in the world. Complimented by a wide variety of exotic spices and vegetables, enhanced by local wines and delicious accompanied by traditional ingredients such as rice and pasta, chicken is the perfect foundation for many dishes. These days, many exotic ingredients are easily obtainable, and it is fun to prepare an international chicken dish for either an informal party or family meal.

Chicken Tacos

Serves 4

	Metric	Imperial	American
Minced chicken	450 g	1 lb	4 cups
Onion, chopped	1	1	1
Red chilli, finely chopped	1	1	1
Salt			
Tomatoes, peeled and chopped	450 g	1 lb	1 lb
Tomato purée	30 ml	2 tbsp	2 tbsp
Taco shells	8	8	8
Cheddar cheese, grated	50 g	2 oz	½ cup

Heat the oil in a large frying pan and cook the onions until translucent. Add the chilli and fry for 2 minutes with a pinch of salt. Stir in the minced chicken and cook for 6 minutes until evenly browned. Stir in the chopped tomatoes and tomato purèe. Cover and simmer for 30 minutes. Arrange the taco shells open side up on a serving dish and fill with the chicken mixture. Sprinkle over the cheese and serve at once.

Chicken Peking

Serves 4

	Metric	Imperial	American
Cooked chicken, chopped	350 g	12 oz	3 cups
Onion, chopped	100 g	4 oz	1 cup
Butter	50 g	2 oz	1/4 cup
Mustard powder	10 ml	2 tsp	2 tsp
Plain (all-purpose) flour	50 g	2 oz	1/2 cup
Chicken stock	300 ml	1/2 pt	1 1/4 cups
Milk	150 ml	1/4 pt	2/3 cup
Chopped fresh parsley	2 tbsp	2 tbsp	2 tbsp
Salt	2.5 ml	1/2 tsp	1/2 tsp
Noodles:			
Egg noodles	225 g	8 oz	1/2 lb
Butter	25 g	1 oz	2 tbsp

In a pan fry the chopped onion in the butter until golden. Add the mustard and flour and cook for 1 minute without browning. Blend in the stock and milk for 3–5 minutes, then add the parsley and season to taste with salt. Add the chicken and heat through.

Cook the noodles according to the manufacturers instructions. Once cooked drain and rinse in cold water then return to the pan, with the butter, and shake them gently over a low heat until piping hot. Arrange the noodles on a serving dish with the chicken on top, and serve immediately.

Chicken Marengo

Serves 4

	Metric	Imperial	American
Chicken joints	4	4	4
Butter	50 g	2 oz	¼ cup
Oil	15 ml	1 tbsp	1 tbsp
Onion, chopped	1	1	1
Plain (all-purpose) flour	15 g	½ oz	1 tbsp
Dry white wine	85 ml	3 fl oz	5½ tbsp
Tomato purée	15 ml	1 tbsp	1 tbsp
Chicken stock	300 ml	½ pt	1¼ cups
Garlic clove	1	1	1
Bay leaf	1	1	1
Seasoning			
Mushrooms, sliced	100 g	4 oz	2 cups

Heat the oil and butter in a heavy frying pan or flameproof casserole. When the butter stops foaming, put in the washed and dried joints and fry them on all sides until golden. Remove from the casserole and set aside. In the same pan, cook the chopped onion until it is soft and golden, about 4–5 minutes, then sprinkle in the flour and let it brown for 1 minute. Pour in the wine and let it bubble for a minute, then add all the remaining ingredients, except the mushrooms. Return the chicken to the casserole, cover and cook in a pre-heated oven at 190°C/375°F/gas mark 5 for 45 minutes or until the chicken is tender. Test by piercing the dark part of the leg with a knife–it should cut easily and show no pink flesh. Ten minutes before serving, add the sliced mushrooms. If the sauce is too thin (it should be the consistency of pouring cream), remove the lid and cook rapidly for 5 minutes on the hob. Then lower the heat and simmer for 10 minutes to allow the sauce to reduce and thicken.

Deep South Chicken

Serves 4

	Metric	Imperial	American
Cooked chicken, chopped	1	1	1
Onion, chopped	1	1	1
Mushrooms	3	3	3
Streaky bacon rashers (slices)	100 g	4 oz	⅔ cup
Green (bell) peppers	2	2	2
Oil	60 ml	4 tbsp	4 tbsp
Tomatoes, peeled and chopped	4	4	4
Seasoning			
Clear honey	90 ml	6 tbsp	6 tbsp
White wine	60 ml	4 tbsp	4 tbsp
Chicken stock	600 ml	1 pt	2½ cups
Plain (all-purpose) flour	50 g	2 oz	½ cup

Lightly fry the onion, mushrooms, bacon and peppers in the oil. Remove them from the frying pan and arrange in a casserole with the chopped tomatoes. Season, then add the honey, wine and stock to the frying pan and bring to the boil. Pour the mixture into the casserole dish. Cover and cook in a pre-heated oven, 180°C/350°F/gas mark 4, for 30 minutes. Strain and set aside the vegetables. Place the sauce in a pan and thicken with the flour. Add the chopped chicken and vegetables to the sauce and continue cooking for 5 –10 minutes before serving.

Chicken Pizzaiola

Serves 4

	Metric	Imperial	American
Minced chicken	450 g	1 lb	1 lb
Oil	30 ml	2 tbsp	2 tbsp
Onions, chopped	2	2	2
Garlic cloves, chopped	2	2	2
Chopped fresh oregano	10 ml	2 tsp	2 tsp
Stock	150 ml	¼ pt	⅔ cup
Dry sherry	30 ml	2 tbsp	2 tbsp
Seasoning			
Butter	5 ml	1 tsp	1 tsp
Spaghetti	225 g	8 oz	½ lb
Double (heavy) cream	150 ml	¼ pt	⅔ cup
Grated Parmesan cheese, to serve			

Heat the oil in a large saucepan and fry the onions and garlic until golden. Add the oregano and the chicken and continue to cook, stirring, for 8 minutes. Lower the heat and simmer for 25 minutes. Add the stock and sherry and season to taste. Bring a large pan of water to the boil, stir in the butter and add the spaghetti. Cook for 7–8 minutes until the spaghetti is cooked but firm. Gradually stir the cream into the minced chicken. Drain the spaghetti and pour into a hot dish. Pour over the chicken mince and serve immediately with a dish of grated Parmesan cheese and a green salad.

Portuguese Chicken

Serves 4

	Metric	Imperial	American
Chicken legs	8	8	8
Butter	50 g	2 oz	¼ cup
Onion	1	1	1
Tomatoes, peeled	3	3	3
Seasoning			
Grated cheese	40 g	1½ oz	3 tbsp

Melt the butter and brown the chicken in a casserole. Slice the onion thinly and arrange over the chicken. Slice the tomatoes add them to the casserole. Season well and sprinkle with grated cheese. Cover and cook in a pre-heated oven at 190°C/375°F/gas mark 5 for 30 minutes. Remove the lid and return to the oven for 10 minutes to brown. Serve hot with rice.

Hungarian Chicken Paprika

Serves 4

	Metric	Imperial	American
Chicken joints	4	4	4
Seasoned flour	40 g	1½ oz	3 tbsp
Onions, chopped	225 g	8 oz	2 cups
Butter	50 g	2 oz	¼ cup
Paprika	15 ml	1 tbsp	1 tbsp
Tomato juice	150 ml	¼ pt	⅔ cup
Sugar	5 ml	1 tsp	1 tsp
Salt	5 ml	1 tsp	1 tsp
Bay leaf	1	1	1
Yoghurt or soured (dairy sour) cream	150 ml	¼ pt	⅔ cup

Skin the chicken joints and toss them in the seasoned flour. Fry the chopped onions very gently in butter for 3 minutes until soft, but not brown. Move them to one side of the pan. Add the chicken and fry until golden for 5–7 minutes. Combine the paprika, tomato juice, sugar and salt and pour them over the chicken. Add the bay leaf. Cover the pan and simmer for 45–60 minutes. Transfer the chicken to a warm dish, remove the bay leaf and stir the yoghurt or soured cream into the sauce and reheat gently, without boiling, for 2–3 minutes. Pour over the chicken. Serve with potatoes, rice or dumplings.

Parisian Chicken

Serves 4

	Metric	Imperial	American
Chicken	1.5 kg	3 lb	3 lb
Back bacon	100 g	4 oz	⅔ cup
Chicken livers	100 g	4 oz	1 cup
Onion, small	1	1	1
Butter	75 g	3 oz	⅓ cup
Brandy	30 ml	2 tbsp	2 tbsp
Garlic clove	1	1	1
Fresh breadcrumbs	50 g	2 oz	1 cup
Grated lemon rind	1	1	1
Seasoning			
Egg	1	1	1

Bone the chicken or ask the butcher to do it for you. Chop the bacon, chicken livers and onion finely and fry them in half the butter until soft and golden, but not brown. Pour in the brandy. Crush the garlic and add it to the pan, with the breadcrumbs, lemon rind and seasoning, and bind it with the egg. Push the stuffing into the boned chicken, secure the opening and mould the bird into shape. Grease a piece of foil with the remaining butter and wrap the chicken in it. Simmer it in boiling water for 1 hour and then let it cool in the water. Carve downwards so everyone gets a portion of chicken and stuffing. Serve with salad and new potatoes.

Chicken Cacciatore

Serves 4

	Metric	Imperial	American
Chicken joints	*4*	*4*	*4*
Seasoning			
Oil	*30 ml*	*2 tbsp*	*2 tbsp*
Onion, chopped	*1*	*1*	*1*
Garlic clove	*1*	*1*	*1*
Tomatoes	*3*	*3*	*3*
Mushrooms	*50 g*	*2 oz*	*1 cup*
Chicken stock	*45 ml*	*3 tbsp*	*3 tbsp*
Tomato purée (paste)	*15 ml*	*1 tbsp*	*1 tbsp*
Sherry	*15 ml*	*1 tbsp*	*1 tbsp*

Season the chicken joints, in a pan, fry the chicken in the oil for 10 minutes until golden. Add the chopped onion and crushed garlic and cook until the onion is soft and golden. Drain off any excess oil. Peel and chop the tomatoes and slice the mushrooms. Add them to the pan and stir in the stock, tomato purée and sherry. Cover and simmer for 45 minutes.

Chicken Niçoise

Serves 4

	Metric	Imperial	American
Cooked chicken, finely chopped	350 g	12 oz	3 cups
Olive oil	45 ml	3 tbsp	3 tbsp
Onion, chopped	1	1	1
Mushrooms, sliced	100 g	4 oz	2 cups
Chopped fresh parsley	30 ml	2 tbsp	2 tbsp
Seasoning			
Chicken stock	600 ml	1 pt	2½ cups
Creamed tomatoes	225 g	8 oz	1 cup
Macaroni	350 g	12 oz	3 cups
Butter	50 g	2 oz	¼ cup

Heat the oil in a pan. Add the onion and mushrooms and cook gently for 10 minutes. Add the parsley, seasoning, stock and creamed tomatoes. Stir well, bring to the boil, then simmer until the mixture has thickened and reduced in volume. Cook the macaroni in a large pan of boiling, salted water for 10 minutes. Drain well, and then toss in the melted butter. Add the chicken to the sauce and bring to boiling point. Pile the macaroni onto a serving dish or bowl, make a well in the centre and pour in the chicken mixture.

Maryland Kebabs
with Mushroom Sauce

Serves 4

	Metric	Imperial	American
Marinade			
Soft brown sugar	25 g	1 oz	2 tbsp
Worcestershire sauce	15 ml	1 tbsp	1 tbsp
Lemon juice	30 ml	2 tbsp	2 tbsp
Salt			
Kebabs			
Chicken breasts	2–4	2–4	2–4
Baby onions	8	8	8
Streaky bacon rashers (slices)	6	6	6
Bananas	3	3	3
Red (bell) pepper, seeded	1	1	1
Sauce			
Butter	25 g	1 oz	2 tbsp
Onion, chopped	1	1	1
Flat mushrooms, chopped	175 g	6 oz	3 cups
Plain (all-purpose) flour	15 g	½ oz	1 tbsp
Beef stock	300 ml	½ pt	1¼ cups
Single (light) cream	60 ml	4 tbsp	4 tbsp
Worcestershire sauce	15 ml	1 tbsp	1 tbsp
Seasoning			

Blend together the marinade ingredients. Cut the chicken into 5 cm (2 in) cubes and toss in the marinade allow to stand, covered, for 4 hours in a cool place or 2 hours in the refrigerator. Place the

onions in a pan of boiling water and simmer for 10 minutes. Stretch the bacon on a board with the back of a round-bladed knife and cut each rasher in half. Drain the chicken and reserve the marinade. Cut each banana into 4, wrap each piece in a bit of bacon and dip in the marinade. Cut the peppers into 2.5 cm (1 in) squares.

Assemble the chicken, bacon-wrapped bananas, onions and red pepper alternately on 4 skewers. Brush with marinade and place under a moderately hot grill for 7 minutes, then turn them and grill for a further 7 minutes, basting once with marinade. Serve the kebabs on a bed of boiled rice.

For the sauce, melt the butter in a pan and gently fry the onion for 5 minutes. Add the mushrooms and cook for 2 minutes. Stir in the flour and cook for 1 minute. Remove from the heat and blend in the stock. Return to the heat and bring to the boil, stirring. Simmer for 3 minutes and stir in the cream and Worcestershire sauce. Season and serve hot with the kebabs. This recipe works equally well if chicken wings are used instead of chicken breast meat.

Chicken Pilaff

Serves 4

	Metric	Imperial	American
Chicken portions	4	4	4
Butter	75 g	3 oz	6 tbsp
Red wine or dry cider	150 ml	¼ pt	⅔ cup
Redcurrant jelly	15 ml	1 tbsp	1 tbsp
Almonds or cashew nuts	25 g	1 oz	¼ cup
Pilaff			
Dried apple rings	3	3	3
Dried apricots	50 g	2 oz	⅓ cup
Onion, chopped	1	1	1
Butter	40 g	1½ oz	3 tbsp
Long-grain rice	225 g	8 oz	1 cup
Chicken stock	750 ml	1¼ pts	3 cups
Seasoning			
Currants	50 g	2 oz	⅓ cup

Soak the dried apple rings and apricots overnight.

Pre-heat the oven to 180°C/350°F/gas mark 4. Spread the chicken portions with 50 g (2 oz/4 tbsp) butter and put them in a roasting tin. Pour half the wine or cider over them. Roast them for 35 minutes, raising the heat to 200°C/400°F/gas mark 6 for the last 5 minutes to brown them thoroughly.

Meanwhile, prepare the pilaff. Using a flameproof casserole, cook the onion in 25 g (1 oz) butter until just coloured. Add the rice and stir well. Add 600 ml (1 pt/2½ cups) stock, season and bring to the boil. Cover and put the casserole in the oven on a shelf below the chicken dish for 12 minutes, or until barely cooked. While the rice is cooking, stew the apricots and apple rings for 10 minutes in the water in which they have been soaking. Drain them and cut into pieces. Add the currants. Stir the fruit carefully into the rice with a fork. If necessary, moisten with a little stock. Season well and dot with the remaining butter. Cover with foil and a lid and replace in the oven on a low shelf. Leave for 15–20 minutes, forking the rice over once or twice. When the rice is dry, remove it from the oven.

Remove the chicken from the oven and set the chicken aside. Make up the gravy in the roasting pan using the remaining red wine or cider and some of the stock. Add the redcurrant jelly and boil. Fry the nuts in the remaining butter until brown. Serve the chicken portions on the rice. Spoon a little gravy over each piece, serving the remainder in a sauceboat. Scatter the nuts over the chicken and serve hot.

Chicken Pompadour

Serves 4

	Metric	Imperial	American
Cooked chicken	350 g	12 oz	¾ lb
Spaghetti	225 g	8 oz	½ lb
Seasoning			
Butter	50 g	2 oz	¼ cup
Single (light) cream	150 ml	¼ pt	⅔ cup
Egg yolk	1	1	1
Chopped fresh parsley	5 ml	1 tsp	1 tsp
Tomato sauce			
Olive oil	30 ml	2 tbsp	2 tbsp
Onion, chopped	1	1	1
Garlic clove, crushed	1	1	1
Herbs, mixed dried	15 ml	1 tbsp	1 tbsp
Tomatoes, creamed	450 g	1 lb	2 cups
Seasoning			

Cook the spaghetti in boiling salted water until just tender. Drain. Grease a basin with half the butter and line it with two-thirds of the spaghetti. Chop the chicken, season and mix with the cream, egg yolk and parsley. Put into the spaghetti-lined basin and top with the remaining spaghetti. Cover with foil and place over a pan of gently simmering water for 1 hour.

Meanwhile, make the tomato sauce by frying the onion and garlic in the olive oil. Add the creamed tomatoes and herbs and season. Stir and leave to simmer on a very low heat to allow the flavours to develop. Turn the spaghetti out onto a hot dish and serve with the tomato sauce.

Poona Chicken

Serves 4

	Metric	Imperial	American
Chicken joints	4	4	4
Chicken stock	600 ml	1 pt	2½ cups
White wine	30 ml	2 tbsp	2 tbsp
Seasoning			
Curry sauce			
Onion, small	1	1	1
Butter	15 g	½ oz	1 tbsp
Oil	15 ml	1 tbsp	1 tbsp
Curry powder	30 ml	2 tbsp	2 tbsp
Curry paste	5 ml	1 tsp	1 tsp
White wine	150 ml	¼ pt	⅔ cup
Lemon juice			
Salt			
Sugar			
Mayonnaise			
Apricot or apple purée	45 ml	3 tbsp	3 tbsp
Yoghurt	150 ml	¼ pt	⅔ cup
Cold cooked rice	450 g	1 lb	4 cups
Canned pineapple cubes	225 g	8 oz	½ lb
Canned red pepper	150 g	5 oz	1¼ cups
Paprika			
Split toasted almonds	50 g	2 oz	½ cup

Poach the chicken in the stock, wine and seasoning for 30 minutes. Remove the meat from the bones and allow to cool.

To prepare the sauce, fry the onion gently in a pan with the butter and oil until transparent.

Add curry powder and paste to taste, depending on strength of the seasoning and how you like your curry, and cook for 2–3 minutes. Stir in the wine, the stock used to poach the chicken and lemon juice, adding sugar and salt to taste. Cook without a lid over a medium heat for 15 minutes so that the liquid reduces a little. Strain and leave to cool. Beat the cooled liquid into the mayonnaise, adding apricot or apple purèe to give a good coating consistency. Finally beat in the yoghurt. Adjust the seasoning, then pour the sauce over the chicken and toss well. Chill slightly.

Meanwhile, mix the cold rice with the cubes of pineapple and strips of red pepper. Arrange around the edge of a serving dish and pile the chicken in the centre. Dust with paprika and toss the toasted almonds over the chicken before serving.

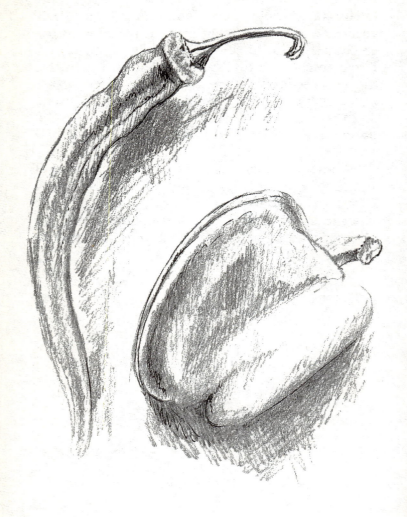

Alabama Chicken

Serves 4

	Metric	Imperial	American
Chicken joints	4	4	4
Plain (all-purpose) flour	25 g	1 oz	2 tbsp
Salt	5 ml	1 tsp	1 tsp
Curry powder	5 ml	1 tsp	1 tsp
Oil for frying			
Bananas	2	2	2
Streaky bacon rashers (slices)	4	4	4
Canned sweetcorn	350 g	12 oz	3 cups
Dessicated (shredded) coconut	30 ml	2 tbsp	2 tbsp

Mix together the flour, salt and curry powder and use to coat the chicken joints. Cook the joints in oil for 10 minutes, turning once or twice until golden. Cover and continue cooking for 15 minutes. Peel the bananas, cut them in half lengthwise and then across to make four pieces. Add the banana pieces and bacon rashers to the fat. Cook for 5 minutes. Heat the corn in a separate pan and then drain off the liquid. Arrange the corn on a serving dish and put the chicken pieces on top. Surround with the banana and bacon and sprinkle over the coconut.

Spring Rolls with Chicken

Serves 4

	Metric	Imperial	American
Minced chicken	75 g	3 oz	¾ cup
Oil	1 tbsp	1 tbsp	1 tbsp
Spring onions (scallions), chopped	3	3	3
Stick of celery, chopped	1	1	1
Cooked prawns	50 g	2 oz	½ cup
Canned water chestnuts, chopped	3	3	3
Bean sprouts	50 g	2 oz	½ cup
Cooked long-grain rice	75 g	3 oz	¾ cup
Soy sauce	10 ml	2 tsp	2 tsp
Honey	5 ml	1 tsp	1 tsp
Large ready-made pancakes	8	8	8
Egg, beaten	1	1	1
Oil for frying			

Heat the oil in a large pan and cook the onion and celery until soft. Add the chicken and water chestnuts and cook for 5 minutes. Chop the prawns roughly and add to the meat with the bean sprouts. Stir in the rice and cook until the meat is well browned. Add the soy sauce and honey, stirring all the time. Remove from the heat. Spoon equal amounts of the mixture into the centre of each pancake and brush the edges with beaten egg. Fold in the sides and roll up to form a parcel. Seal all the edges with egg. Heat the oil in a deep pan and fry the rolls two at a time, until crisp and golden. Drain on kitchen paper and serve hot.

Neapolitan Chicken

Serves 4

	Metric	Imperial	American
Chicken joints	4	4	4
Seasoned flour			
Olive oil	45 ml	3 tbsp	3 tbsp
Lemon juice	30 ml	2 tbsp	2 tbsp
Seasoning			
Grated Parmesan cheese	50 g	2 oz	½ cup
Breadcrumbs	25 g	1 oz	½ cup
Oil for frying			
Spaghetti	175 g	6 oz	⅜ cup
Butter			

Coat the chicken joints lightly with seasoned flour. Mix together the olive oil, lemon juice, salt and pepper. Pour this over the chicken and leave for 1 hour. Mix three-quarters of the cheese with the breadcrumbs and coat the chicken joints with it. Fry the chicken in hot oil for 25 minutes, turning it as necessary. Meanwhile, cook the spaghetti in boiling salted water for 10–15 minutes or until tender. Drain and toss in the butter and remaining cheese. Put the spaghetti in a serving dish and arrange the chicken pieces on top. Serve with freshly cooked fennel.

SAUCY CHICKEN

The delicate flavour of chicken is the perfect foil for richly-flavoured sauces. Fruit, barbecue, curry, cream, wine and mushroom sauces are all good, either as sauces to cook the chicken in, or to mix with cooked chicken. Boiled rice, mashed potatoes or new potatoes are ideal accompaniments to contrast with these sauces, or the dishes may be served with crusty bread and a green salad.

Chicken in Sherry Sauce

Serves 4

	Metric	Imperial	American
Chicken joints	4	4	4
Seasoning			
Butter	50 g	2 oz	¼ cup
Green (bell) peppers	2	2	2
Dry sherry	90 ml	6 tbsp	6 tbsp
Chopped fresh thyme	15 ml	1 tbsp	1 tbsp
Lemon			

Season the chicken joints and cook them in a large pan in the butter on a low heat for 5 minutes on each side. Cut the peppers into neat strips and add them to the pan. Cook for 15 minutes, turning frequently until the chicken is tender and lightly brown. Arrange the chicken on a serving dish and keep it warm. Pour the sherry into the pan juices, stir well and then pour over the chicken. Sprinkle with the thyme and garnish with lemon quarters. Serve with new potatoes and mangetout (snowpeas).

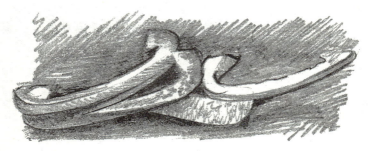

Golden Fruited Chicken

Serves 4

	Metric	Imperial	American
Chicken joints	4	4	4
Rosé wine	300 ml	½ pt	1¼ cups
Honey	30 ml	2 tbsp	2 tbsp
Butter	50g	2 oz	¼ cup
Dried apricots	100 g	4 oz	⅔ cup
Seasoning			

Wipe the chicken joints and put them into a dish with the wine. Leave in a cold place for 2 hours. Remove the chicken from the wine and dry it thoroughly. Mix the honey and butter together and spread generously on the chicken pieces, reserving about one-quarter of the mixture. Put the apricots into a bowl, pour some boiling water over and leave them to stand for 10 minutes then drain. Put the wine in the bottom of a casserole and add the apricots and the chicken joints. Cover and cook at 180°C/350°F/gas mark 4 for 45 minutes. Take out the chicken pieces and put them cut side down on a grilling rack.

Season, then brush with the reserved honey mixture and grill until golden. Serve with the apricot and wine sauce on a bed of saffron rice.

Saucy Chicken

Serves 4

	Metric	Imperial	American
Chicken joints	4	4	4
Seasoning			
Butter	25 g	1 oz	2 tbsp
Made mustard	10 ml	2 tsp	2 tsp
Cayenne pepper	1.5 ml	1/4 tsp	1/4 tsp
Tomatoes, skined and chopped	4	4	4
Oil	15 ml	1 tbsp	1tbsp
Onion, chopped	4	4	4
Garlic, crushed	2	2	2

Brush the joints with melted butter, then season and cook them under a hot grill for 3–4 minutes each side. Reduce the heat and grill them for a further 7 minutes each side, or until cooked through. Meanwhile, mix the mustard, and cayenne pepper together. Fry the onions and crushed garlic with the oil for 2 minutes. Add the chopped tomatoes and cook rapidly for 10 minutes. Stir in the mustard and cayenne pepper mix.

As soon as the chicken is ready, spread half the mixture over each joint, put them back under a medium-hot grill and cook for 2 minutes. Serve with sautèed potatoes and a salad. Heat the remaining mustard mixture and serve as a sauce.

Chicken in Yoghurt Sauce

Serves 4

	Metric	Imperial	American
Chicken portions	4	4	4
Butter	15 g	½ oz	1 tbsp
Onion	1	1	1
Green (bell) pepper	1	1	1
Seasoning			
Natural yoghurt	300 ml	½ pt	1¼ cups
Plain (all-purpose) flour	15 g	½ oz	1 tbsp

Grease an ovenware dish with the butter. Slice the onion into rings and put them on the base of the dish. Put the chicken portions on top. Cut the stem from the pepper, remove the seeds and cut the flesh into rings. Arrange the rings on the chicken and season well with salt and pepper. Pour over the yoghurt, cover with foil or a lid and cook at 190°C/375°F/gas mark 5 for 1 hour. Blend the flour with a little water until smooth. Add a little hot liquid from the chicken and mix well, then add to the dish. Continue cooking uncovered for 20 minutes. Serve with Jerusalem artichokes and tomatoes,.

Slimmers' Orange Chicken

Serves 4

	Metric	Imperial	American
Chicken quarters	4	4	4
Butter	15 g	½ oz	1 tbsp
Onion, small	1	1	1
Orange, large	1	1	1
Worcestershire sauce	30 ml	2 tbsp	2 tbsp
Tomato purée	5 ml	1 tsp	1 tsp
Seasoning			
Dill, chopped			

Melt the butter in a pan and gently fry the finely-chopped onion for 5 minutes until soft and golden. Pare thin strips of peel from half the orange with a potato peeler, and cut it into 'match-sticks'. Grate the remaining orange rind and squeeze out the orange juice. Add the orange match-sticks, grated rind and juice to the onion with the Worcestershire sauce and tomato purèe. Bring to the boil and season to taste. Put the chicken quarters on to a large piece of foil in a roasting tin, and spoon the orange sauce over. Cover completely in foil and bake at 200°C/400°F/gas mark 6 for 30 minutes. Uncover and bake for a further 15 minutes or until golden brown. Spoon the roasting juices over the chicken to serve and garnish with chopped dill. The chicken quarters are also delicious eaten cold with salad.

Chicken in Mushroom Sauce

Serves 4

	Metric	Imperial	American
Chicken joints	4	4	4
Oil	15 ml	1 tbsp	1 tbsp
Butter	25 g	1 oz	2 tbsp
Onion	1	1	1
Mushrooms, sliced	225g	8 oz	½ lb
Seasoning			
Milk	150 ml	¼ pt	⅔ cup
Single (light) cream	45 ml	3 tbsp	3 tbsp
Lemon juice	5 ml	1 tsp	1 tsp
Cornflour (cornstarch)	10 ml	2 tsp	2 tsp

Fry the chicken joints in a large pan with the oil and butter until golden, turning them from time to time. Chop the onion and cook in the oil until soft, stir in the mushrooms and cook for 8 minutes. Blend the cornflour and milk together and stir into the mushrooms. Cook for 2 minutes, season, then pour over the chicken. Cover and simmer for 30 minutes, stirring occasionally. Stir in the cream and lemon juice. Season again with freshly ground pepper before serving.

Chicken with Curry Sauce

Serves 4

	Metric	Imperial	American
Chicken joints	4	4	4
Seasoning			
Butter	25 g	1 oz	2 tbsp
Oil	30 ml	2 tbsp	2 tbsp
Sauce			
Butter	25 g	1 oz	2 tbsp
Plain flour	25 g	1 oz	2 tbsp
Medium curry powder	10 ml	2 tsp	2 tsp
Seasoning			
Pinch of garlic salt			
Stock	300 ml	½ pt	1¼ cups
Single (light) cream	200 ml	7 fl oz	1 cup

Season the chicken and, in a large pan fry the joints in butter and oil very gently for 15 minutes on each side. Meanwhile, make the sauce. Melt the butter in a small pan and stir in the flour and curry powder. Mix in the salt and pepper, garlic salt and stock and simmer for 5 minutes. Take off the heat, stir in the cream and serve with the fried chicken.

Chicken in Lemon Sauce

Serves 4

	Metric	Imperial	American
Chicken joints	4	4	4
Seasoned flour	50 g	2 oz	½ cup
Butter	50 g	2 oz	¼ cup
Olive oil	30 ml	2 tbsp	2 tbsp
White wine	300 ml	½ pt	1¼ cups
Chicken stock	300 ml	½ pt	1¼ cups
Lemon	1	1	1
A little saffron powder			
Single (light) cream	30 ml	2 tbsp	2 tbsp
Seasoning			
Black and green olives			
Paprika for garnish			

Toss the chicken joints in seasoned flour and, in a large pan, fry them slowly in the butter and oil until golden brown. Stir in the remaining flour and cook for 1 minute. Add the wine and chicken stock, and the lemon cut into slices. Transfer to a flameproof casserole. Cover and cook over a low heat for 40 minutes or until the chicken is tender. Lift on to a warm serving dish. Stir the saffron into the liquid. Cool it slightly and add the cream. Adjust the seasoning. Pour the sauce over the chicken and garnish with black and green olives. Dust with paprika. Serve with new potatoes.

Chicken and Barbecue Sauce

Serves 4

	Metric	Imperial	American
Chicken	4	4	4
Seasoning			
Oil	30 ml	2 tbsp	2 tbsp
Butter	25 g	1 oz	2 tbsp
Onion, chopped	1	1	1
Tomato purée	10 ml	2 tsp	2 tsp
Plain (all-purpose) flour	10 ml	2 tsp	2 tsp
Mustard powder	10 ml	2 tsp	2 tsp
Soft brown sugar	25 g	1 oz	2 tbsp
Water	150 ml	¼ pt	⅔ cup
Vinegar	30 ml	2 tbsp	2 tbsp
Worcestershire sauce	30 ml	2 tbsp	2 tbsp

Season the chicken joints and brush them with the oil. Remove the grid from the grill pan and grill the chicken under a high heat, turning as necessary, for about 12 minutes each side. Melt the butter in a pan and cook the chopped onion until soft. Stir in the tomato purée and cook for 2 minutes. In a bowl, mix the flour, mustard, sugar, water, vinegar and Worcestershire sauce to a smooth cream and stir into the onion and tomato mixture. Simmer for 10 minutes and serve with the grilled chicken.

Grapefruit Chicken

Serves 4

	Metric	Imperial	American
Chicken quarters	4	4	4
Seasoned flour			
Butter	50 g	2 oz	¼ cup
Oil	30 ml	2 tbsp	2 tbsp
Brandy	15 ml	1 tbsp	1 tbsp
Chicken stock	150 ml	¼ pt	⅔ cup
Sherry	60 ml	4 tbsp	4 tbsp
Seasoning			
Grapefruit	1	1	1

Dust the chicken with the flour and, in a large pan, brown the chicken quarters in the butter and oil until golden. Reduce the heat and cook the chicken gently until tender. Drain off the fat. Pour on the brandy and touch it with a lighted match. Let the flames subside then remove the chicken to a serving dish, keeping it hot. Add the chicken stock, sherry and seasoning to the pan. Cut the grapefruit in half and squeeze in the juice of one half. Stir well and cook until the liquid is reduced to half the original volume. Remove the segments from the second half of the grapefruit and skin them. Stir the segments into the sauce and pour over the chicken quarters.

Honey Curry Chicken

Serves 4

	Metric	Imperial	American
Chicken	1.5 kg	3 lb	3 lb
Lemon	½	½	½
Onion, chopped	2	2	2
Garlic, crushed	1	1	1
Oil	15 ml	1 tbsp	1 tbsp
Tomatoes, skinned and chopped	450 g	1 lb	1 lb
Seasoning			
Clear honey	225 g	8 oz	¾ cup
Medium curry powder	15 ml	1 tbsp	1 tbsp
Long-grain rice	100 g	4 oz	½ cup
Double (heavy) cream	150 ml	¼ pt	⅔ cup
Lemon juice			

Roast the chicken with the lemon inside at 180°C/350°F/gas mark 4 for 1¼ hours. Allow to cool, then divide into joints. Fry the onion and garlic in a large saucepan with the oil for 2 minutes. Add the tomatoes and simmer for 20 minutes. Add the honey and stir in the curry powder. Season to taste. Bring to the boil, simmer over a low heat for 10 minutes and then cool. Boil the rice in a separate pan until tender. Rinse under cold water and leave in a colander to drain. Line a serving dish with the rice and arrange the chicken joints on top. Fold the cream and lemon juice into the cold honey-curry sauce and spoon it over the chicken. Serve with desiccated (shredded) coconut and popadums as side dishes.

Curried Chicken with Rice

Serves 4

	Metric	Imperial	American
Chicken joints	4	4	4
Oil	30 ml	2 tbsp	2 tbsp
Butter	25 g	1 oz	2 tbsp
Onion, chopped	225 g	8 oz	½ lb
Plain (all-purpose) flour	15 g	½ oz	1 tbsp
Medium curry powder	25 g	1 oz	2 tbsp
Chicken stock	600 ml	1 pt	2½ cups
Eating apple, chopped	1	1	1
Sultanas	100 g	4 oz	⅔ cup
Seasoning			
Long-grain rice	225 g	8 oz	1 cup

In a large pan fry the chicken in oil and butter until golden then remove from the pan and keep warm. Fry the onions in the pan until golden and soft then stir in the flour and curry powder and fry for 2 minutes. Add the stock, chopped apple, sultanas and seasoning, and stir well. Return the chicken joints to the pan, bring to the boil and simmer gently for 45 minutes. Cook the rice in boiling salted water for 12 minutes or until tender, drain well and serve with the chicken. Mango chutney and other traditional Indian side dishes go well with this curry.

CHICKEN PIES

Short-crust or puff pastry both make delicious chicken pies, whether served in deep dishes, individual patty tins or sandwich tins. Pastry is a clever extra ingredient which extends leftover cold chicken especially when made combined with say, a creamy sauce, bacon or mushrooms, plenty of herbs and seasoning. Fillo pastry cups (page 90) make another ideal snack where leftover chicken can be assembled in advance and the dish prepared just before serving.

Chicken Plate Pie

Serves 4

	Metric	Imperial	American
Cooked chicken	450 g	1 lb	1 lb
Eggs	2	2	2
Milk	150 ml	¼ pt	⅔ cup
Tarragon	5 ml	1 tsp	1 tsp
Grated rind ½ lemon			
Seasoning			
Shortcrust pastry	350 g	12 oz	¾ lb

In a bowl beat together the eggs and milk until well blended. Add the tarragon, lemon rind, salt and pepper and the chicken cut into dice. Reserve one-third of the pastry then roll out the remainder to a 23 cm (9 in) circle. Use it to line an 18 cm (7 in) sandwich tin, leaving a small overlap. Fill it with the chicken mixture and dampen the edges of the pastry. Roll out the remaining pastry into a 20 cm (8 in) circle and cover the pie. Seal the edges and flute them. Make six 2.5 cm (1 in) slits from the centre of the pie and fold them back to make a star. Bake at 220°C/425°F/gas mark 7 for 20 minutes. Reduce heat to 180°C/350°F/gas mark 4 and bake for a further 30 minutes. Serve hot or cold.

Filo Chicken Morsels

Serves 4

	Metric	Imperial	American
Filo cups:			
Filo pastry	6 sheets	6 sheets	6 sheets
Butter	25 g	1 oz	2 tbsp
Filling:			
Cooked minced chicken	225 g	8 oz	2 cups
Olive oil	5 ml	1 tsp	1 tsp
Garlic clove, crushed	½	½	½
Ginger root, peeled and finely grated	2.5 cm	1 inch	1 inch
Crème fraîche	60 ml	4 tbsp	4 tbsp
Chopped fresh chives	30 ml	2 tbsp	2 tbsp
Seasoning			

Cut the filo pastry into 6 cm (2½ inch) squares, cutting through all 6 sheets at a time, so that you make eighteen 6-layer squares. Brush each layer with melted butter, and then place the 6 layers of each square in a hole in a pattie tin. The holes should be very small to suit the size of the squares. If you have a larger pattie tin, use larger squares. Press the pastry layers into the base of each hole and spread out the edges. Fill each hole with greaseproof paper and baking beans or crumpled foil and bake at 200°C/400°F/gas mark 6 for 8 minutes. Remove the baking beans or foil and allow to cool on a wire rack. The small filo cups will be very fragile and should be handled with care.

To make the filling; heat the olive oil and fry the garlic for 1 minute. Add the ginger and fry again for 1 minute, stirring. Blend in the chicken and blend in the créme fraîche, chives and seasoning. Cook for 2 minutes, stirring all the time until the chicken is very hot. Spoon gently into the filo cups and serve immediately, or prepare the filling earlier in the day, keep refrigerated and assemble 5 minutes before required. Garnish with tiny slivers of radish.

Summer Chicken Pie

Serves 4

	Metric	Imperial	American
Chicken	1.5 kg	3 lb	3 lb
Water	300 ml	½ pt	1¼ cups
Worcestershire sauce	30 ml	2 tbsp	2 tbsp
Bay leaves	2	2	2
Peppercorns	6	6	6
Sprig of parsley			
Sprig of thyme			
Onion	1	1	1
Cloves	6	6	6
Carrot, chopped	1	1	1
Plain (all-purpose) flour	275 g	10 oz	2½ cups
Mixed lard and butter	150 g	5 oz	⅔ cup
Pinch of salt			
Cold water	45 ml	3 tbsp	3 tbsp
Cooked bacon or ham, chopped	150 g	6 oz	1 cup
Milk or beaten egg for glazing			

Put the chicken into a large pan with the water, Worcestershire sauce, bay leaves, peppercorns, parsley, thyme, onion spiked with the cloves, and carrot. Cover with a tightly fitting lid, bring to the boil and simmer gently for 50 minutes or until tender. Reserve the stock and set aside the chicken to cool, then remove the meat and chop it coarsely. Make the pastry by sifting the flour and salt together, then rubbing in the fats until the mixture is like fine breadcrumbs. Add enough water to mix to a firm dough. Turn on to a floured surface and knead it lightly until smooth. Cut off quarter and reserve for lid. Roll out remainder into a circle 30 cm (12 in) in diameter. Line an 18 cm (7 in) sandwich tin, joining the seam. Place half the chopped chicken in the base of the pie, adding the chopped bacon or ham and cover it with the remaining chicken. Spoon over 45 ml (3 tbsp) of the chicken stock. Roll out the remaining pastry to a 17.5 cm (7 in) circle to make a lid. Cover the pie, trim and seal the edges, and leave a small hole in the centre of the crust. Brush with milk or beaten egg. Bake at 200°C/400°F/gas mark 6 for 30 minutes, then reduce the temperature to 180°C/350°F/gas mark 4 for 30 minutes. If the top of the pie browns too quickly, cover it with foil. Leave the pie in the tin to cool. When it is nearly cold, pour a little stock through the hole in the centre of the lid and leave it in a cold place until set.

Chicken Lattice Pie

Serves 4

	Metric	Imperial	American
Cooked chicken, finely chopped	225 g	8 oz	½ lb
White sauce	300 ml	½ pt	1¼ cups
Button mushrooms, thinly sliced	100 g	4 oz	2 cups
Seasoning			
Puff pastry	350 g	12 oz	¾ lb
Beaten egg to glaze			

Mix the sauce with the finely-chopped chicken, thinly-sliced mushrooms and seasoning, and leave to cool. Roll out the pastry 30 x 20 cm (12 x 8 in). Cut it in half across and roll each piece of pastry to a rectangle 30 x 18 cm (12 x 7 in). Put one half on a baking tray and pile the chicken filling down the centre. Fold the other piece of pastry in half across the width and use a sharp knife to make cuts on the folded edge to within 2.5 cm (1 in) of the cut edges. Open out the pastry and place it on top of the chicken filling. Seal the edges with beaten egg and use the egg to glaze the top. Bake at 220°C/425°F/gas mark 7 for 40 minutes. Serve hot with vegetables or cold with salad.

Chicken and Sausage Pie

Serves 4

	Metric	Imperial	American
Pork sausages	225 g	8 oz	½ lb
Pinch of mixed herbs			
Butter	25 g	1 oz	2 tbsp
Cooked chicken, chopped	350 g	12 oz	3 cups
Plain flour	25 g	1 oz	2 tbsp
Chicken stock	300 ml	½ pt	1¼ cups
Seasoning			
Shortcrust pastry	350 g	12 oz	¾ lb
Beaten egg to glaze			

Skin the sausages and mix the meat with the herbs. Form the meat into 8 balls and, in a pan fry them in half the butter until golden. Place in a pie dish with the chopped chicken. Pour off half the fat, add the remaining butter and work in the flour. Blend in the stock and bring it to the boil. Stir well and season to taste. Pour into the pie dish and cool. Cover with the pastry and brush with the beaten egg. Bake at 220°C/425°F/gas mark 7 for 40 minutes.

Party Chicken Pie

Serves 4

	Metric	Imperial	American
Chicken	1.5 kg	3 lb	3 lb
Carrot	1	1	1
Onion	1	1	1
Bay leaves	2	2	2
Salt			
A few peppercorns			
Chicken liver from giblets			
Cooked ham	225 g	8 oz	½ lb
Butter	40 g	1½ oz	3 tbsp
Plain (all-purpose) flour	40 g	1½ oz	3 tbsp
Chicken stock	300 ml	½ pt	1¼ cups
White wine	300 ml	½ pt	1¼ cups
Egg yolk	1	1	1
Single (light) cream	15 ml	1 tbsp	1 tbsp
Squeeze of lemon juice			
Chopped fresh parsley	15 ml	1 tbsp	1 tbsp
Seasoning			
Puff pastry	225 g	8 oz	½ lb
Beaten egg to glaze			

Rinse and wipe the chicken. Place it in a large pan with the carrot, onion, bay leaves, salt, peppercorns, chicken liver and water to cover. Bring to the boil, then simmer for 1–1¼ hours until the chicken is tender. Remove from the heat and allow to cool in the liquid for 15 minutes. Lift out the chicken and remove the flesh from the bones. Measure 300 ml (½ pt/1¼ cups) skimmed and strained chicken stock for the sauce (use the remainder for soup). Cut the ham into cubes. Melt the butter in a saucepan, stir in the flour and remove from the heat. Gradually add the chicken stock, then the wine. Bring to the boil, stirring until the sauce is smooth and thick. Remove from the heat, cool, add the egg yolk, cream, lemon juice, parsley and seasoning to taste. Fill a pie dish with the chicken meat, ham and cooked sauce. Cover it with a pastry lid and decorate with pastry leaves. Leave in the refrigerator to rest for 30 minutes. Brush with beaten egg to glaze. Cook at 230°C/450°F/gas mark 8 for 10 minutes.

Reduce heat to 200°C/400°F/gas mark 6 and continue cooking for a further 20–25 minutes until the filling is heated through and the pastry golden.

Chicken Flan

Serves 4

	Metric	Imperial	American
Shortcrust pastry	225 g	8 oz	½ lb
Onion, small	1	1	1
Eating apple	1	1	1
Butter	15 g	½ oz	1 tbsp
Curry powder	15 g	½ oz	1 tbsp
Eggs, beaten	2	2	2
Milk	150 ml	¼ pt	⅔ cup
Salt			
Cooked chicken	225 g	8 oz	2 cups

Roll out the pastry to line a 20 cm (8 in) flan ring. Chop the onion and apple and cook in the butter for 5 minutes over a low heat. Add the curry powder and stir it over the heat for 1 minute. Cool then mix with the beaten eggs, milk and salt. Cut the chicken into small dice and arrange it in the pastry case. Pour on the curry mixture and bake at 200°C/400°F/gas mark 6 for 35 minutes. Serve hot or cold.

Chicken and Potato Pie

Serves 4

	Metric	Imperial	American
Cooked chicken	450 g	1 lb	1 lb
Potatoes	450 g	1 lb	1 lb
Chicken stock	300 ml	½ pt	1¼ cups
Evaporated milk	300 ml	½ pt	1¼ cups
Seasoning			
Chopped fresh parsley	15 g	1 tbsp	1 tbsp
Puff pastry	350 g	12 oz	¾ lb

Cut the chicken and potatoes into small cubes.
Mix the stock, evaporated milk, seasoning and
parsley and put into a pie dish. Cover with the
pastry and bake at 220°C/425°F/gas mark 7 for 40
minutes.

CHICKEN SALADS

Everyone loves chicken salad with crisp lettuce leaves or tangy fruit in a creamy well-season dressing. To contrast with the white chicken flesh, introduce some colourful vegetables or fruit, or chopped ham to the salad. Serve in a glass dish, or in individual portions arranged on lettuce leaves. A little chopped parsley or mint, or a sprinkling of chopped nuts makes a tasty and attractive finish.

Chicken Salad Veronique

Serves 4

	Metric	Imperial	American
Cooked chicken	350 g	12 oz	3 cups
Green grapes	175 g	6 oz	3/8 lb
Olive oil	30 ml	2 tbsp	2 tbsp
Lemon juice	5 ml	1 tsp	1 tsp
Grated lemon rind	1.5 ml	1/4 tsp	1/4 tsp
Seasoning			
Single (light) cream	60 ml	4 tbsp	4 tbsp
Crisp lettuce leaves			
Tomatoes	2	2	2
Basil, finely chopped	15 ml	1 tbsp	1 tbsp

Cut the chicken into bite-sized pieces and mix with the halved and seeded grapes. Combine the oil, lemon juice and rind, seasonings and cream, then stir this dressing into the chicken and grape mixture. Cover it and set aside in a refrigerator to allow the flavours to blend. To serve, line a shallow bowl with lettuce leaves, pile the chicken salad into the centre and garnish with thin wedges of tomato and finely chopped basil.

Summer Salad

Serves 4

	Metric	Imperial	American
Long-grain rice	100 g	4 oz	½ cup
Cooked peas	100 g	4 oz	1 cup
French dressing			
Cooked chicken portions	4	4	4
Lettuce			
Fresh grapefruit sections			
Cherries or strawberries	100 g	4 oz	¼ lb
Black grapes	100 g	4 oz	¼ lb
Peaches	2	2	2
Feather Cream Dressing			
Egg white	1	1	1
Soured (dairy sour) cream	150 ml	¼ pt	⅔ cup
Mayonnaise	150 ml	¼ pt	⅔ cup
Salt			
Paprika	10 ml	2 tsp	2 tsp

Cook and drain the rice then add the peas and enough French dressing to moisten. Pile it into the centre of a dish and chill. Arrange the chicken portions on the rice. Surround with crisp lettuce leaves and fill with the fruits. Make the dressing by whisking the egg white until very stiff and folding in the cream, mayonnaise, salt and paprika. If possible, make it in advance so that the paprika will colour the dressing a delicate pink. Use a little of the sauce to coat the chicken and serve the rest in a sauce boat.

Sunshine Salad

Serves 4

	Metric	Imperial	American
Mayonnaise	60 ml	4 tbsp	4 tbsp
Vinaigrette	15 ml	1 tbsp	1 tbsp
Double (heavy) cream	150 ml	¼ pt	⅔ cup
Cooked chicken	350 g	12 oz	¾ lb
Orange	1	1	1
Eating apple	1	1	1
Cucumber	5 cm	2 in	2 in
Spring onion	1	1	1
Seasoning			
Lettuce leaves	4	4	4

Mix the mayonnaise and vinaigrette. Whip the cream to soft peaks and mix in the mayonnaise mixture. Chop the chicken into neat dice. Peel the orange and divide it into segments. Do not peel the apple, but cut it into quarters, remove the core and cut them into neat slices. Dice the cucumber and slice the spring onion. Mix the chicken, orange, apple, cucumber and onion into the cream and season with salt and pepper to taste. Arrange 4 portions on a bed of chopped lettuce leaves on individual plates and serve with buttered rice.

Spring Salad

Serves 4

	Metric	Imperial	American
Long-grain rice	175 g	6 oz	¾ cup
Small packet frozen peas or mixed vegetables	1	1	1
Sultanas	50 g	2 oz	⅓ cup
Cooked chicken	350 g	12 oz	¾ lb
Mayonnaise	90 ml	6 tbsp	6 tbsp
Top of the milk	60 ml	4 tbsp	4 tbsp
Mild curry powder	1.5 ml	¼ tsp	¼ tsp
Salt	2.5 ml	½ tsp	½ tsp
Watercress			
Tomatoes			

Boil the rice in a pan of salted water. Cook for 5 minutes, then add the vegetables and sultanas and cook for a further 7 minutes. Drain and leave to cool. Chop the chicken into neat pieces and mix with the rice and vegetables. Mix the mayonnaise, milk, curry powder and salt and pour it over the rice mixture. Stir thoroughly and put into a salad bowl. Garnish with watercress and tomato wedges.

Chicken Terrine

Serves 4

	Metric	Imperial	American
Minced chicken	450 g	1 lb	1 lb
Stock	150 ml	1/4 pt	2/3 cup
Gelatine	15 g	1/2 oz	1 tbsp
Cooked ham, chopped	50 g	2 oz	1/2 cup
Breadcrumbs	25 g	1 oz	1/2 cup
Thyme, chopped	5 ml	1 tsp	1 tsp
Chilli powder	1.5 ml	1/4 tsp	1/4 tsp
Small red (bell) pepper, very finely chopped	1	1	1
Seasoning			

Pour the stock into a small heat-proof bowl and sprinkle over the gelatine. Allow to soak for 5 minutes. Stand bowl in a pan of hot water to melt the gelatine. Place the remaining ingredients in a large bowl and blend together. Pour in the gelatine mixture and blend again. Press the mixture into a 450 g (1 lb) loaf tin 18 x 7.5 cm (7 x 3 in) and refrigerate until firm. Heat the sides of the tin with a tea towel rung out in hot water for 1 minute and then turn out.

Chicken Salad Caprice

Serves 4

	Metric	Imperial	American
Cooked chicken	350 g	12 oz	¾ lb
Large ripe banana	1	1	1
Lemon juice	30 ml	2 tbsp	2 tbsp
Large orange	1	1	1
Mayonnaise	45 ml	3 tbsp	3 tbsp
Double (heavy) cream	30 ml	2 tbsp	2 tbsp
Crisp lettuce leaves			
Black grapes	100 g	4 oz	¼ lb

Slice the banana into a bowl and turn it over and over in the lemon juice. Peel the orange removing the skin and pips from the segments and add to the bowl. Add the chicken cut into 1 cm (½ in) dice, the mayonnaise and the cream. Mix together lightly, cover and set aside in the fridge to allow the flavours to blend. To serve, line a shallow bowl with lettuce leaves, pile the chicken salad in the centre and garnish with the halved and seeded grapes.

Virginia Chicken Salad

Serves 4

	Metric	Imperial	American
Medium dessert apples	2	2	2
Lemon juice	45 ml	3 tbsp	3 tbsp
Double (heavy) cream	60 ml	4 tbsp	4 tbsp
Mayonnaise	30 ml	2 tbsp	2 tbsp
Salt	1.5 ml	1/4 tsp	1/4 tsp
Cooked chicken, chopped	350 g	12 oz	3/4 lb
sticks of celery	4	4	4
Walnuts	15 g	1 tbsp	1 tbsp
Crisp lettuce leaves			
Small red-skinned apple	1	1	1
Sprigs of parsley			

Peel and core the apples, cut them into dice and toss with 15 ml (1 tbsp) lemon juice. Lightly whip the cream and stir into it the mayonnaise, salt and 15 ml (1 tbsp) lemon juice. Add the diced apple, chicken, celery and walnuts. Mix, cover and set aside in the fridge. To serve, arrange the lettuce leaves around a flat dish and pile the chicken salad in the centre. Cut the unpeeled red-skinned apple into slices and dip them in the remaining lemon juice. Garnish the salad with the apple slices and parsley sprigs, then serve.

Danish Chicken Cocktail

Serves 4

	Metric	Imperial	American
Cooked chicken	350 g	12 oz	¾ lb
Mayonnaise	300 ml	½ pt	1¼ cups
Tomato purée	30 ml	2 tbsp	2 tbsp
Lemon juice	30 ml	2 tbsp	2 tbsp
Worcestershire sauce	5 ml	1 tsp	1 tsp
Curry powder	5 ml	1 tsp	1 tsp
Seasoning			
Small lettuce	1	1	1
Cucumber	¼	¼	¼
Tomato	1	1	1

Cut the chicken into neat strips. Mix the mayonnaise with the tomato purèe, lemon juice, Worcestershire sauce, curry powder, salt and pepper. Stir in the chicken carefully. Shred the lettuce very finely and dice the cucumber, leaving the skin on. Mix the lettuce and cucumber and arrange in four individual bowls or glasses. Pile the chicken mayonnaise on top and garnish with the tomato cut in quarters.

Chicken and Chestnut Salad

Serves 4

	Metric	Imperial	American
Cooked chicken	350 g	12 oz	¾ lb
Cooked chestnuts	100 g	4 oz	½ cup
Sticks of celery	2	2	2
Hard-boiled (hard cooked) eggs	2	2	2
Spanish stuffed olives	8	8	8
Mayonnaise	300 ml	½ pt	1¼ cups
Lettuce leaves			

Chop the chicken in small pieces then chop the chestnuts and celery. Slice the eggs and olives, reserving two for garnishing. Mix the chicken, chestnuts, celery, eggs and sliced olives carefully in the mayonnaise. Arrange on the lettuce leaves and garnish with the reserved olives, quartered. This is a good dish at Christmas when chestnuts are easily available. Sprinkle over 15 ml (1 tbsp) finely chopped chervil if available.

Chicken and Pineapple Salad

Serves 4

	Metric	Imperial	American
Canned pineapple	175 g	6 oz	medium can
Olive oil	15 ml	1 tbsp	1 tbsp
Lemon juice	15 ml	1 tbsp	1 tbsp
Finely-grated lemon rind	1.5 ml	1/4 tsp	1/4 tsp
Pineapple juice	30 ml	2 tbsp	2 tbsp
Salt	1.5 ml	1/4 tsp	1/4 tsp
Cooked chicken	350 g	12 oz	3/4 lb
Chopped mint	5 ml	1 tsp	1 tsp
Crisp lettuce leaves	8	8	8
Cherry tomatoes to garnish			
Basil	15 ml	1 tbsp	1tbsp

Drain the pineapple pieces and chop them finely. Prepare the dressing in a large basin by mixing together the oil, lemon juice, lemon rind, pineapple juice and salt. Add the chicken, cut into dice and the pineapple pieces. Cover and set it aside in a refrigerator to allow the flavours to blend. Shortly before serving stir in the chopped mint and divide the salad among the cupped lettuce leaves. Arrange around a flat serving dish and garnish the centre with cherry tomatoes and a sprinkling of fresh basil.

Chicken and Cucumber Salad

Serves 4

	Metric	Imperial	American
Cooked chicken	350 g	12 oz	¾ lb
Cucumber, large	1	1	1
Single (light) cream	30 ml	2 tbsp	2 tbsp
Mayonnaise	30 ml	2 tbsp	2 tbsp
Lemon juice	10 ml	2 tsp	2 tsp
Chopped fresh mint	5 ml	1 tsp	1 tsp
Salt			
Tomatoes	2	2	2
Hard-boiled (hard cooked) egg	1	1	1

Cut the cucumber in half. Thinly slice one half, and cut the other half into small cubes. Cut the chicken into small pieces. Prepare the dressing by mixing the cream, mayonnaise, lemon juice, mint and salt together, and then stir in the chopped cucumber and chicken. Set aside in a cool place for an hour for the flavours to blend. When ready to serve, pile the chicken in the centre of a flat dish, circle it with cucumber slices and garnish with the sliced tomatoes and hard-boiled egg.

Crunchy Summer Salad

Serves 4

	Metric	Imperial	American
Cooked chicken	450 g	1 lb	1 lb
Hard-boiled (hard cooked) eggs	2	2	2
Green (bell) pepper	1	1	1
Tomatoes, skinned	3	3	3
Cauliflower	225 g	8 oz	½ lb
Small lettuce	1	1	1
Olive oil	150 ml	¼ pt	⅔ cup
Lemon juice	60 ml	4 tbsp	4 tbsp
Chopped fresh mint	5 ml	1 tsp	1 tsp
Seasoning			
Stuffed green olives	12	12	12

Cut the chicken into match-stick sized pieces. Slice the eggs, green pepper and skinned tomatoes. Break the raw cauliflower into small florets and shred the lettuce. Mix the oil, lemon juice, mint and seasoning, and leave it to stand for 1 hour. Put all the salad ingredients into a serving bowl. Slice the olives and add to salad. Mix the dressing well, pour it over the salad and toss lightly before serving.

LEFTOVER CHICKEN

A little leftover chicken makes a marvellous second-day dish. There need be no waste, for chicken meat is lean. Use minced chicken to make croquettes, patties or a mousse, or chopped for use in sandwiches, pancakes or vol-au-vent cases. If the chicken carcass is simmered in water to make stock, this will give added flavour to second-day dishes and can be used as the basis for delicious and nourishing soups.

Chicken Chilli Crunch

Serves 4

	Metric	Imperial	American
Minced chicken	450 g	1 lb	1 lb
Onion	1	1	1
Garlic clove, crushed	1	1	1
Green (bell) pepper, seeded and finely chopped	1	1	1
Tomatoes, skinned and chopped	225 g	8 oz	2 cups
Chilli powder	5 ml	1 tsp	1 tsp
Green chilli	1	1	1
Seasoning			
Parmesan cheese, grated	50 g	2 oz	½ cup

Fry the chicken for 1 minute then add the onion and garlic clove. Continue to cook, stirring, for 5 minutes before adding the green pepper, tomatoes, chilli powder and green chilli. Stir well and season with salt and pepper. Spoon the mixture into an ovenproof dish and sprinkle with cheese. Place under the grill until the cheese is brown and serve with sautèed potatoes.

Chicken Pancakes

Serves 4

	Metric	Imperial	American
Cooked chicken	225 g	8 oz	½ lb
Plain (all-purpose) flour	100 g	4 oz	1 cup
Pinch of salt			
Egg	1	1	1
Milk	300 ml	½ pt	1¼ cups
Cooked peas	225 g	8 oz	2 cups
Butter	15 g	1 tbsp	1 tbsp
Flour	7.5 ml	1½ tsp	1½ tsp
Crème fraîche	75 ml	5 tbsp	5 tbsp
Seasoning			
Parmesan cheese	15 ml	1 tbsp	1 tbsp

Sift the flour and salt into a basin. Add the egg and half the milk and beat well until smooth. Add the rest of the milk. Lightly grease a frying pan and make thin pancakes with the batter. Cut the chicken into small dice and mix with the peas. Heat the butter in a saucepan and stir in the flour. Cook for 1 minute and blend in the créme fraîche. Season well. Mix the chicken and créme fraîche mixtures together and put a little in the centre of each pancake, roll up and arrange in a greased ovenware dish. Heat at 180°C/350°F/gas mark 4 for 20 minutes. Sprinkle over the parmesan cheese and place under the grill to brown.

Danish Chicken Soup

Serves 4

	Metric	Imperial	American
Chicken stock	1. 2 litre	2 pts	5 cups
Eggs	2	2	2
Curry powder	10 ml	2 tsp	2 tsp

Heat the stock to boiling point. Beat the eggs and curry powder with a fork and add to the hot stock, stirring carefully with a fork. Serve at once.

Chunky Chicken Patties

Serves 4

	Metric	Imperial	American
Minced chicken	450 g	1 lb	1 lb
Butter	15 g	1 tbsp	1 tbsp
Flour	7.5 ml	1½ tsp	1½ tsp
Milk, warm	75 ml	5 tbsp	5 tbsp
Seasoning			
Cheese, grated	50 g	2 oz	½ cup
Egg yolks	3	3	3
Flour for coating			
Oil for frying			

Melt the butter in a small pan and stir in the flour. Cook for 1 minute, stirring constantly gradually adding the milk. Cook until the sauce thickens then season with salt and pepper. Blend in the minced chicken, cheese and egg yolks and form into 12 round shapes. Dip in the flour and re-shape if necessary. Heat the oil and fry the patties until golden brown on both sides. Drain on paper towels and serve hot with sautèed potatoes and courgettes, or use to fill buttered crusty rolls.

Chicken Croquettes

Serves 4

	Metric	Imperial	American
Cooked chicken	350 g	12 oz	3 cups
Butter	25 g	1 oz	2 tbsp
Plain (all-purpose) flour	25 g	1 oz	1 tbsp
Chicken stock or milk	150 ml	¼ pt	⅔ cup
Mushrooms, chopped	50 g	2 oz	1 cup
Chopped fresh parsley	5 ml	1 tsp	1 tsp
Seasoning			
Egg	1	1	1
Breadcrumbs			
Oil for frying			

Mince the chicken finely. Melt the butter, blend in the flour and gradually add the stock or milk and stir continuously over a low heat. Add the chopped mushrooms and parsley and cook for 3 minutes. Season well and stir in the chicken, mixing well. Turn on to a plate to cool. Divide into 16 equal-sized pieces and roll into sausage shapes. Coat the croquettes with beaten egg and breadcrumbs and fry them in hot fat until golden and hot right through.

Crunchy Chicken Pie

Serves 4

	Metric	Imperial	American
Chicken mince	450 g	1 lb	1 lb
Onion, chopped	1	1	1
Garlic clove, crushed	1	1	1
Tomatoes, skinned and chopped	225 g	8 oz	2 cups
Tomato purée	15 ml	1 tbsp	1 tbsp
Chopped fresh tarragon	5 ml	1 tsp	1 tsp
Seasoning			
Tortilla chips	100 g	4 oz	1/4 lb
Parmesan cheese, grated	50 g	2 oz	1/2 cup

Fry the onion and crushed garlic for 1 minute.
Add the chicken and cook, stirring continuously,
for 5 minutes. Stir in the tomatoes, tomato purèe
and tarragon. Blend well and season with salt
and pepper. Continue cooking, stirring from time
to time for 15 minutes. Spoon the chicken into an
ovenproof dish. Crumble the tortilla chips and
mix with the cheese. Top the chicken with the
mixture. Place under the grill until the cheese is
brown. Serve with green vegetables.

Leek and Potato Soup

Serves 4

	Metric	Imperial	American
Onion	1	1	1
Leeks	4	4	4
Potatoes	3	3	3
Butter	50 g	2 oz	¼ cup
Chicken stock	1.2 litres	2 pts	5 cups
Seasoning			
Single (light) cream	30 ml	2 tbsp	2 tbsp

Chop the onion finely. Clean the leeks well and cut them into rings. Peel and dice the potatoes. Melt the butter in a large pan and cook the vegetables over a low heat for 5 minutes. Add the stock and season well. Cover and simmer for 45 minutes until the vegetables are soft. Stir in the cream and serve hot. If preferred, the soup may be sieved or liquidized before adding the cream. If the smooth soup is chilled and sprinkled with chopped fresh chives, it becomes Vichyssoise.

Fried Chicken Sandwiches

Serves 4

	Metric	Imperial	American
Cooked chicken	350 g	12 oz	¾ lb
Seasoning			
Pinch of nutmeg			
Chopped fresh parsley	5 ml	1 tsp	1 tsp
White sauce	90 ml	6 tbsp	6 tbsp
Egg yolk	1	1	1
Bread slices	8	8	8
Milk	300 ml	½ pt	1¼ cups
Eggs	2	2	2
Breadcrumbs			
Oil for frying			

Chop the chicken finely and mix it with the salt, pepper, nutmeg, parsley, white sauce and egg yolk. Make sandwiches with this mixture and cut each one in half. Beat together the milk, eggs and a little salt and pepper. Dip the chicken sandwiches into this, coat them with breadcrumbs and fry in hot oil until golden. Medium-thick bread slices are best for these sandwiches. Serve with salad or pickles.

Chicken and Spinach Bake

Serves 4

	Metric	Imperial	American
Minced chicken	450 g	1 lb	1 lb
Fresh spinach	450 g	1 lb	1 lb
Seasoning			
Nutmeg, grated	5 ml	1 tsp	1 tsp
Tarragon, chopped	5 ml	1 tsp	1 tsp
Nutmeg, ground	5 ml	1 tsp	1 tsp
Cottage cheese	225 g	8 oz	1 cup
Natural yoghurt	300 ml	½ pt	1¼ cups
Eggs, beaten	2	2	2
Butter for greasing			

Wash and drain the spinach then place in a large saucepan without any water and cover with a lid. Cook over a gentle heat for 10 minutes. Strain in a sieve, pressing to remove excess water. Return to a bowl and season with pepper and ground nutmeg. Season the chicken with the tarragon, salt and pepper then place alternate layers of spinach, cottage cheese and chicken in a greased ovenproof dish. Beat together the yoghurt and eggs and pour over the chicken. Sprinkle with grated nutmeg and bake at 180°C/350°F/gas mark 4 for 50 minutes until golden on top.

Chicken Mousse

Serves 4

	Metric	Imperial	American
Cooked chicken	225 g	8 oz	½ lb
Chicken stock	300 ml	½ pt	1¼ cups
Gelatine	10 g	¼ oz	½ tbsp
Double (heavy) cream	150 ml	¼ pt	⅔ cup
Seasoning			
Cucumber and tomato to garnish			

Mince the chicken twice using the smallest cutter or blend in a liquidiser. Crush the chicken carcass then place in a large pan. Add vegetables and herbs for flavouring, barely cover with water and simmer for about 1 hour. Strain the stock and reduce it to 250 ml (8 fl oz/1 cup). Dissolve the gelatine in the stock and add half to the chicken meat. Whisk the cream until fluffy but not stiff. Fold in the chicken and seasoning. Transfer to a glass dish and chill until set. Pour half the remaining jellied stock on top. Arrange a simple decoration of cucumber and tomato and then cover it with the rest of the stock. Chill before serving with a green salad and walnut oil dressing.

Chicken Party Sticks

Serves 4

	Metric	Imperial	American
Minced chicken	450 g	1 lb	1 lb
Pork sausagemeat	225 g	8 oz	½ lb
Fresh breadcrumbs	50 g	2 oz	1 cup
Chopped fresh thyme	10 ml	2 tsp	2 tsp
Garlic clove, crushed	1	1	1
Egg, beaten	1	1	1
Tabasco sauce	15 ml	1 tbsp	1 tbsp
Onion, finely chopped	1	1	1

Place all the ingredients in a bowl and blend together well. Roll 1 tablespoon into a small ball the size of a walnut and place on a greased baking sheet. Continue to do the same with the rest of the mixture. Bake in a pre-heated oven at 200°C/400°F/gas mark 6 for 15 minutes. Push each ball onto wooden skewers and serve with a piquant or tomato dip.

Victorian Chicken Toasts

Serves 4

	Metric	Imperial	American
Cooked chicken	350 g	12 oz	3 cups
White sauce	300 ml	½ pt	1¼ cups
Onion	1	1	1
Butter	25 g	1 oz	2 tbsp
Cooked potato	225 g	8 oz	½ lb
Toast slices			
Chopped chives			
Paprika pepper			

If possible, make the white sauce with chicken stock and then stir in the diced chicken. Chop the onion very finely and cook it in the butter until soft and golden. Stir the onion and diced potato into the chicken mixture and heat through. Serve hot on toast, sprinkled with chopped chives, and the merest dusting of paprika pepper.

INDEX